INNOVATION
~~without~~
DRAMA

6-step formula to implement digital innovation and drive explosive growth in traditional business

ALAN CAMPOS

Copyright © 2024 Alan Campos
All Rights Reserved
ISBN: 9798327665644

DEDICATION

To my parents and sister, who laid the foundation of everything I am today with immense sacrifice, dedication, and values that I will carry forever. And to my beloved wife, who has always supported me and was essential for me to develop my professional skills, career, and the method described in this book.

A BIT OF CONTENT

HOW IT ALL BEGAN	10
THE OPPORTUNITY	13
THE 6-STEP METHOD	14

1. YOUR REASON TO INNOVATE

THE AGE OF DIGITAL INNOVATION	19
1. TYPES OF INNOVATION	19
1.1. Incremental Innovation	20
1.2. Sustaining Innovation	23
1.3. Disruptive Innovation	25
1.4. Radical Innovation	28
2. OTHER TYPES OF INNOVATION	32
2.1. Product Innovation	32
2.2. Service Innovation	33
2.3. Process Innovation	31
2.4. Business Model Innovation	34
2.5. Technological Innovation	34
2.6. Marketing Innovation	35
2.7. Organizational Innovation	35
2.8. Social Innovation	36
2.9. Architectural Innovation	37
2.10. Modular Innovation	37
3. THE CRITICAL ROLE FOR EXECUTIVE ALIGNMENT	38

3.1. Understand the Real Motivation	38
3.2. Map Common Transformation Drivers	39
WORKING SESSION	**41**

What is Digital Innovation for Your Company?

2. DIGITAL EVOLUTION

ASSESSING THE DIGITAL INNOVATION MATURITY OF YOUR ORGANIZATION	**45**
1. HOW DIGITALLY ADVANCED IS YOUR SECTOR?	45
2. STAGES OF DIGITAL INNOVATION MATURITY	49
WORKING SESSION	**51**

The Digital Innovation Maturity Assessment

3. DIGITAL AMBITION

DEFINING YOUR ORGANIZATION'S DIGITAL FUTURE	**59**
1. BALANCE OPTIMIZATION VS NEW BUSINESS	59
2. DEFINE AN ASPIRATIONAL PURPOSE	61
3. UNDERSTAND THE ORGANIZATIONAL STRUCTURE	62
3.1. Where Should I Put The Digital Innovation Area?	62
3.2. What We Can Learn From Apple's Organizational Structure	65

WORKING SESSION	68

How to Write a Powerful Digital Statement That Resonates?

4. ACTION PLAN

FROM VISION TO ACTION	73
1. START BY MAPPING CUSTOMER'S PAIN POINTS	73
2. UNDERSTAND THE DIFFERENT INNOVATION MODELS	74
2.1. Merger and Acquisitions (M&A)	75
2.2. Corporate Venture Capital	76
2.3. Joint-Venture	77
2.4. Innovation Competitions	78
2.5. R&D Lab	78
2.6. Acceleration Programs	79
2.7. Intrapreneurship Squads	80
2.8. Ideas Management	81
2.9. Open Innovation	81
2.10. Digital Transformation	82
3. DEFINING PILOTS & QUICK WINS	83
3.1. Revisit Your Reason to Innovate	84
3.2. Select The Right Initiative	84

3.3. Scructure it for Success	85

WORKING SESSION	86

Prioritization Tools to Focus on What Really Matters

5. EXECUTION

EXECUTING DIGITAL INNOVATION	93
1. BRING YOUR HEROES	93
1.1. Identify Internal Talent with a Growth Mindset	95
1.2. Blend with External Experts	95
1.3. Mix Industry Expertise	95
1.4. Partner with a Forward-Thinking Talent Acquisition Team	96
1.5. Sell the Vision, Not Just the Role	96
1.6. Be Aspirational in Job Descriptions	96
1.7. Pay Well — They're Heroes, Not Replacements	97
1.8. Protect the Heroes	97
1.9. Reignite Their Fire Regularly	97
2. ORGANIZE THEM INTO SQUADS	98
2.1. Squad Definition and Structure	99
2.2. Operating Principles	100
2.3. Goals and Alignment	100
2.4. Continuous Improvement	101
3. FOLLOW THE 2 PIZZA RULE	101

3.1. Why Smaller Teams Drive Better Innovation … 103

3.2. Amazon's Example … 104

4. IMPLEMENT THE MOONSHOT THINKING … **106**

4.1. What is a Moonshot? … 106

4.2. Advantages … 107

4.3. Beyond Theory … 107

4.4. How to Implement it … 108

4.5. Benefits … 109

5. DEFINE SUCCESS METRICS USING OKRS … **110**

6. SHIFT YOUR ORGANIZATION'S MINDSET … **112**

6.1. From Project to Product … 112

6.2. From Building to Last to Building to Change … 113

6.3. From Big Bang to Baby Steps … 115

7. DON'T OVERENGINEER - SOLVE SMART NOT HARD … **117**

7.1. Lean Startup … 117

7.2. Minimum Viable Products … 119

7.3. Design Thinking, Sprints & Jams … 122

8. MEASURE CUSTOMER SATISFACTION … **127**

8.1. Implementing NPS: A Step-by-Step Guide … 128

8.2. Survey Template … 129

8.3. Actionable Steps for Improvement … 129

9. ALIGN DIGITAL, IT & BUSINESS … **131**

9.1. Evolve IT from Support to Strategic	131
10. DRIVE GROWTH IMPLEMENTING A FUNNEL STRATEGY	**135**
WORKING SESSION	**140**

Time to Set Up Your OKRs

6. OPTMIZATION

PORTFOLIO MANAGEMENT AND CONTINUOUS INNOVATION PROCESS	**149**
1. EXPLORE NEW BUSINESS MODELS	**149**
2. GET TO KNOW PLATFORM STRATEGIES	**151**
3. STRUCTURE A PLANNING & GOVERNANCE PROCESS	**156**
3.1. Break Your Innovation Plan Into Three Horizons	156
3.2. Define Metrics & KPIs For Each Initiative	158
3.3. Measure The Success Rate of Your Initiatives	161
WORKING SESSION	**164**

Map Owners, Effort & Potential Impact

BONUS MATERIAL & WHAT'S NEXT

EXTRA RESOURCES FOR YOU TO SUCCEED	168

1. **MY PERSPECTIVE ON THE GENERATIVE AI IMPACT** — **168**
   - 1.1. Industrial Revolution — 168
   - 1.2. Technological Revolution — 169
   - 1.3. Bridging the Two Revolutions — 171
   - 1.4. Key Takeaways from AI Predictions — 171
2. **DEMYSTIFYING AI FOR NOT-TECH LEADERS** — **174**
   - 2.1. Main types and a brief explanation — 174
   - 2.2. The AI journey and where we are now — 174
3. **HOW TO MASTER GEN AI IMPLEMENTATION** — **175**
4. **WHAT'S NEXT** — **179**
   - 4.1. A Sneak Peek at the Toolkit I Use — 180
   - 4.2. Join my Executive Community — 182
   - 4.3. Let's Connect — 182

ALAN CAMPOS

A BIT OF CONTEXT

HOW IT ALL BEGAN

When I graduated with a degree in Industrial Design in 2003, I left college eager to understand how organizations operate and thrive. That's when my real journey of learning and experience began.

My first job at an advertising agency showed me an outdated model, clearly unprepared for the demands of the digital age.

Determined to explore new possibilities, I dove into the world of entrepreneurship and created Praontem, one of the first online advertising agency platforms in Latin America that connected clients to freelancers, generating much operational efficiency compared to the traditional advertising agency market.

Launched in 2008, the platform was discontinued years later due to my difficulty in scaling the business, but it was a true digital innovation lab for me.

In search of more scalable businesses, I founded Instaquadros, a platform and marketplace that revolutionized the decoration sector, offering customers a gallery of artists and a wide range of printed and personalized artwork and decorative items.

With the support of an acceleration program based in Brazil and the USA (Rio and NYC), I had access to innovation experts from Harvard and Stanford and an international network of mentors that elevated my knowledge to another level and gave me access to practices and tools used by the world's most innovative companies.

We shook up a traditional and consolidated market. Instaquadros was elected one of the 10 most innovative companies of 2013 in

Brazil and was featured in the Brazil Pavilion at Tech Crunch in San Francisco, the world's largest innovation and technology event.

After an acqui-hiring process, I became Business Unit Head at Nice Photos, the largest B2C photographic printing group in Brazil, bridging the gap to the corporate world.

In 2016, I became Head of Digital Products at Nextel, an American multinational. I encountered a management model that was not at all aligned with what I had learned from digital world experts during my accelerator days.

I created the company's first User Experience team, being responsible for user experience and satisfaction across all digital channels.

This changed the company's results in the first year, improving indicators such as:

Reach: increase in customer base

Penetration: more customers adopting the digital platform and ceasing to use traditional service channels

Recognition: apps rated among the best among all telecoms in the world (highlighted in the App Store and Google Play), two awards as the best telecommunications operator in the country, best IT turnaround elected by Gartner, and highlight at the Mobile World Congress (the world's largest telecom event).

This transformation was key to the strategic vision, which materialized with the sale to the largest telecom group in Latin America.

I was then invited to found a Corporate Venture for the Dasa Group, Nexa Digital.

The challenge was to organize health data. We then launched a virtual health wallet that allowed users to organize their exam results in one place, no matter which laboratory you did it in. It was the first product of what would become the largest health data lake in Latin America with over 5 billion data points.

This caught the market's attention and resulted in an invitation to create the digital area of Novartis, in one of the company's 10 largest markets in the world.

At Novartis, I implemented the first business teams using agile methodology, inspired by Spotify's engineering model, the first open innovation hub among all Latin American pharmas, and the industry's first Growth Hacking team in the world. This enabled the launch of 5 brands 35% faster than the average of other launches and an ROI (Return On Investment) in newly created revenue channels of 2.5x in the first year, paying for the entire investment of creating the area and generating profits in channels previously unexplored by the company.

This experience culminated in my transfer as Head of Digital Strategy to Novartis's largest market in the world, the United States, and later promotion as Head of Global Business Transformation Strategy, contributing to Novartis's inclusion in the list of the 50 Most Innovative Companies of 2021.

THE OPPORTUNITY

In recent years, I realized that everything I had learned from entrepreneurship, about the tactics and strategies of the startup world and the world's most innovative companies, was valuable knowledge that had not reached many leaders of traditional companies. And that it's not enough to just copy and paste the strategies. The corporate world has a particular approach and incentive chain, completely different.

Throughout my journey, it became increasingly clear that companies and executives are under more and more pressure to innovate and adapt to new technologies and methods of strategy and management. The knowledge I acquired during my time venturing with technology startups was fundamental to achieving the results I briefly described here. This knowledge is much more valuable to these companies than I imagined. It also became clear that it was not a matter of copying and pasting the techniques of the world's most innovative companies into a corporate and hierarchical environment. It was necessary to understand the incentive chain, decode, and hack the way traditional companies work to then make them more innovative.

Another important point: nothing I learned and applied throughout this journey is taught in educational institutions. If you are a leader and are pressured to innovate in your company, you will not find a practical program in schools, colleges, or even MBAs.

THE 6-STEP METHOD

Having the privilege of living in both worlds (entrepreneur founder of digital businesses and multinational executive) allowed me to decipher the functioning of large companies, find ways to truly implement the strategies of the world's most innovative companies, and create a simple and practical method of approach that demystifies digital innovation for leaders and empowers them to finally drive innovation in their companies.

Every month, dozens of executives ask me how to implement Digital Innovation in their companies or departments. So, I decoded this code, created a method in the form of a practical guide in 6 steps that was tested, validated, and improved throughout my journey in startups and S&P 500 companies from various industries, and today I apply mentoring and advisory programs where I help leaders of renowned companies in the challenges of Innovation and Digital Transformation.

In this book, I invite you to know and apply this method. Welcome to the exciting journey of digital innovation!

In a simple and practical way, by the end of the reading, you will be able to:

- Discover the real reason to innovate in the context you are in
- Understand at what stage of digital innovation maturity your company or department is today
- Build a vision and ambition for innovation

- Know the strategies of the world's most innovative companies and develop an action plan with quick results
- Execute innovation initiatives
- Measure and optimize innovation initiatives

By exploring these six steps, you will dive into a world full of possibilities and discoveries that will revolutionize the way you think, plan, and deliver results in leadership positions.

You will have access to valuable techniques and relevant insights to enhance your skills, find new leadership and revenue models. You will exponentially improve your results, becoming a reference in your segment.

So, get ready to explore the territory of innovation and transform the results of your company and your future as a leader.

Let's get started!

ALAN CAMPOS

1. YOUR REASON TO INNOVATE

TLDR

This chapter lays the groundwork for understanding innovation's multifaceted nature and its pivotal role in digital transformation. By exploring innovation types and reflecting on your company's strategic position, you can craft an approach that is both practical and tailored to your unique challenges and opportunities.

THE AGE OF DIGITAL INNOVATION

This book is a practical guide, and within these pages, I've reserved just enough space to provide the necessary theoretical context and highlight the types of innovation. The focus is on practicality, aiming to equip you with the knowledge and tools to navigate the digital transformation landscape effectively.

1. TYPES OF INNOVATION

Innovation manifests in various forms, each with its unique characteristics and impact. Understanding these types can illuminate the path for your innovation journey, helping you to strategize effectively.

The Innovation Matrix serves as a pivotal tool for categorizing innovations along two critical dimensions: their impact on the market and the technology they employ. This framework outlines four commonly recognized types of innovations, each distinguished by unique characteristics and strategic implications.

Within this guide, we delve into the nuances of these four innovation types, aiming to provide a clear understanding of their differences and potential applications. To enrich this exploration, we include practical examples of each innovation category. These instances offer tangible insights into how each type of innovation can be effectively implemented, showcasing their capacity to transform practices, markets, and industries.

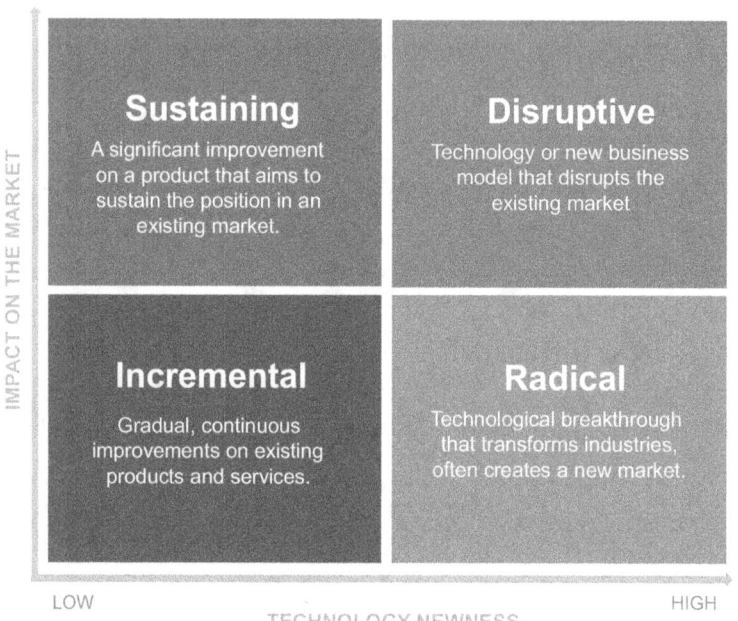

1.1. Incremental Innovation

Incremental innovation represents the most common form of innovation, characterized by gradual and continuous improvements to existing products, services, or processes within the current market. These innovations refine and optimize what already exists without fundamentally altering the core concept or creating new markets. While incremental innovation may not generate industry-shaking changes, it plays a vital role in business sustainability, competitiveness, and efficiency.

Key Characteristics:

- **Gradual advancements** over time rather than sudden breakthroughs.
- **Low risk and low investment**, making it accessible for most businesses.
- **Customer-driven**, responding to user feedback and preferences.
- **Operational efficiency**, improving quality, reducing costs, and increasing performance.

Why Incremental Innovation Matters

Incremental innovation is often overlooked because it lacks the spectacle of disruptive breakthroughs. However, its impact is profound:

Enhancing User Experience – Small but meaningful updates ensure a seamless and improved experience. For example, smartphone manufacturers refine battery life, camera quality, and processing power with each new model.

Cost Efficiency & Resource Optimization – Businesses can maximize the potential of their current infrastructure and expertise instead of investing in radical new developments.

Competitive Differentiation – Even minor improvements can keep a brand ahead of competitors. Consider the continuous refinements in electric vehicle (EV) battery performance, allowing companies like Tesla to maintain industry leadership.

Smoother Adoption & Market Stability – Unlike disruptive innovations that can face resistance, incremental innovation is more easily accepted by customers and stakeholders.

Examples:

TV: The evolution of television technology showcases incremental innovation, with each new model offering slight improvements over the last, such as better picture quality or slimmer designs, without fundamentally changing the concept of television.

Google: Google's search engine algorithms continuously evolve to improve search accuracy, relevance, and speed. Each update builds on existing technology, making the experience better while ensuring stability.

Pharma: In pharmaceuticals, drug companies often refine existing medications to improve effectiveness, reduce side effects, or enhance delivery methods, ensuring that treatments evolve while staying familiar to users.

Incremental innovation is the foundation of sustained progress—an essential strategy for businesses looking to stay relevant, optimize processes, and enhance customer satisfaction without taking unnecessary risks.

1.2. Sustaining Innovation

Sustaining innovation is about enhancing existing products, services, or processes to maintain or strengthen a company's position in the market. Unlike disruptive innovation, which creates new markets, sustaining innovation focuses on improving what already works—refining performance, boosting efficiency, and keeping pace with evolving customer expectations.

Key Characteristics:

- Builds upon existing products to ensure continued relevance.
- Targets mainstream customers who expect better performance without major changes.
- Often driven by market competition and customer demand.
- Helps companies maintain leadership and defend their market share.

Why Sustaining Innovation Matters

Sustaining innovation ensures that businesses remain relevant, competitive, and financially viable in the long run. It plays a critical role in industries where continuous improvement is necessary to prevent obsolescence.

Customer Retention – Meeting customer expectations with frequent improvements fosters loyalty.

Market Leadership – Companies that consistently refine their offerings establish themselves as industry leaders.

Operational Efficiency – Improved processes lower costs and enhance productivity.

Competitive Edge – Keeping up with or outpacing competitors ensures a strong market presence.

Examples:

1st Generation iPhone   iPhone 15 Pro Max

iPhone: The introduction of Face ID, advanced camera systems, and improved battery life in newer iPhone models. These enhancements keep customers engaged while reinforcing brand loyalty without fundamentally altering the product's purpose.

Microsoft: In software, Microsoft's ongoing updates to its Office suite introduce new features and improved performance while keeping the core product familiar. This ensures user adoption while gradually advancing its capabilities.

Sustaining innovation is not about radical reinvention—it's about perfecting and evolving what already works, ensuring long-term market success.

1.3. Disruptive Innovation

Disruptive innovation fundamentally reshapes industries by introducing new products, services, or business models that initially cater to niche markets but eventually displace established market leaders. This type of innovation is often underestimated at first, but as it matures, it outperforms traditional solutions and becomes the dominant force.

Key Characteristics:
- Starts in low-end or unserved markets, often overlooked by industry leaders.

- Initially seen as inferior or non-threatening but improves over time.
- Challenges existing business models and market assumptions.
- Can render traditional players obsolete if they fail to adapt.

Why Disruptive Innovation Matters

Companies that fail to recognize or respond to disruptive innovation risk losing relevance. Understanding and leveraging disruptive innovation can be the key to long-term success and market leadership.

Market Expansion – Disruptive innovations often create entirely new customer segments that were previously unaddressed.

Cost Efficiency – These innovations typically introduce lower-cost alternatives, making services or products more accessible.

Future-Proofing – Organizations that embrace disruptive thinking position themselves for long-term resilience against market shifts.

Technology Advancement – Many disruptive innovations leverage emerging technologies to redefine industries.

Examples:

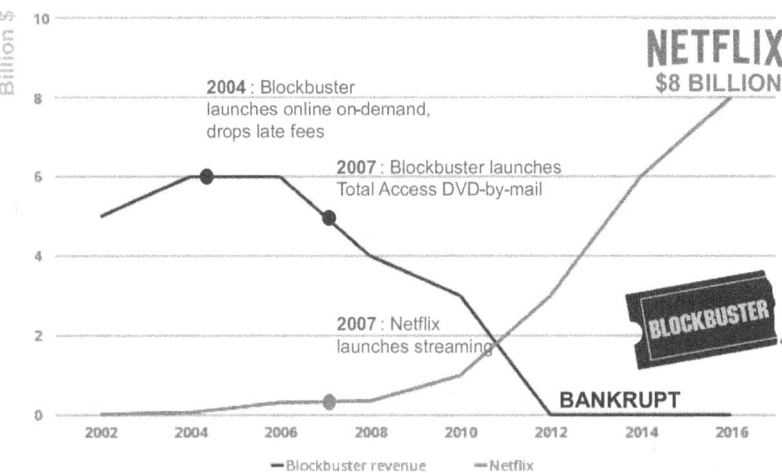

Netflix's rise against Blockbuster is a classic case of disruptive innovation. By leveraging new technology and a unique business model, Netflix transformed the home entertainment industry, making the traditional video rental business model obsolete.

Ride-Sharing Apps (Uber, Lyft) – Taxis dominated urban transportation for decades, but Uber and Lyft disrupted the industry by offering an on-demand, app-based solution that provided greater convenience and competitive pricing.

Digital Photography vs. Film – Kodak, once a market leader in film photography, failed to adapt when digital cameras emerged.

Despite inventing digital photography, Kodak dismissed its potential, ultimately leading to its decline.

Disruptive innovation is about seeing the potential in small, emerging trends and betting on the future. Companies that proactively adapt, invest, and experiment in disruptive opportunities are more likely to lead rather than lag in their industries.

1.4. Radical Innovation

Radical innovation represents breakthroughs that completely transform industries, introducing technologies or business models that were previously unimaginable. Unlike incremental or sustaining innovation, radical innovation does not improve upon existing solutions—it replaces them entirely with something fundamentally new.

Key Characteristics:
- High risk, high reward, often requiring long-term investment and research.
- Revolutionary impact, changing how industries operate or how people interact with products.
- Technological and scientific breakthroughs drive its success.
- Creates entirely new markets or makes existing ones obsolete.

Why Radical Innovation Matters

Radical innovation is the driving force behind major technological and industrial revolutions. While it often faces skepticism and resistance at first, it holds the potential to redefine industries and create entirely new value chains.

Industry Transformation – Radical innovations shift entire industries, forcing competitors to either adapt or disappear.

Exponential Growth Opportunities – When successful, radical innovations lead to unprecedented business expansion.

Long-Term Market Dominance – Companies that pioneer radical innovation often establish themselves as industry leaders for decades.

Reshaping Consumer Behavior – These innovations fundamentally change how people interact with products or services.

Examples:

The Internet – The rise of the internet reshaped communication, commerce, and media, eliminating the need for traditional forms of communication (e.g., fax machines, physical mail for business transactions) and creating entirely new business models like e-commerce and digital advertising.

CRISPR Gene Editing – This breakthrough technology has revolutionized genetic medicine, allowing scientists to edit DNA with precision, opening doors for curing genetic diseases once considered untreatable.

Radical innovation is not about making something slightly better — it is about reinventing industries and unlocking new possibilities that once seemed impossible. It is the rarest and most transformative, driven by revolutionary technology that introduces unprecedented product features. It explores entirely new technologies and often requires significant time and resources. Radical innovations can dramatically transform industries, creating entirely new markets and value networks. They are marked by high uncertainty but have the potential to redefine the competitive landscape.

INNOVATION WITHOUT DRAMA

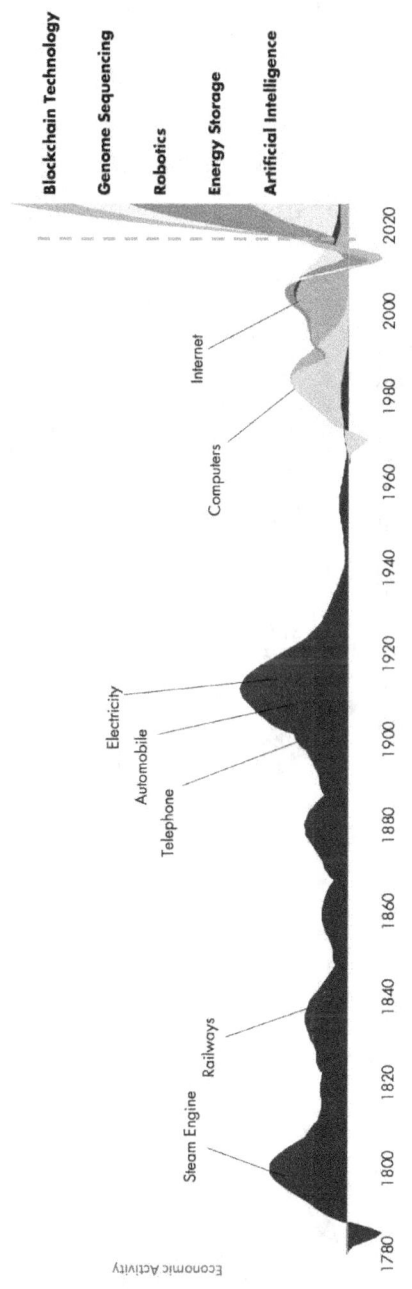

2. OTHER TYPES OF INNOVATION

Beyond the four core categories, there are several other forms of innovation that contribute to business growth, operational efficiency, and competitive advantage. Understanding these additional types can help organizations develop a holistic approach to innovation.

2.1. Product Innovation

Product innovation involves developing new products or significantly improving existing ones to meet customer needs or differentiate in the market.

Key Characteristics:

- Enhances features, performance, or usability.
- Addresses consumer demands or emerging trends.

- Can be incremental, sustaining, disruptive, or radical.

Example: Tesla's introduction of full self-driving capabilities in its electric vehicles, pushing the boundaries of automotive technology.

2.2. Service Innovation

Service innovation focuses on enhancing how services are delivered to improve customer satisfaction and operational efficiency.

Key Characteristics:

- Improves service delivery, personalization, or accessibility.
- Often incorporates digital transformation or automation.
- Can lead to new business models or customer experiences.

Example: Amazon Prime revolutionized e-commerce by offering fast shipping, streaming, and exclusive deals in a bundled subscription.

2.3. Process Innovation

Process innovation optimizes how businesses operate, improving efficiency, reducing costs, and increasing quality.

Key Characteristics:

- Streamlines production, logistics, or operations.
- Enhances productivity and sustainability.
- Often supported by automation and AI.

Example: Toyota's Lean Manufacturing System, which reduced waste and improved efficiency, became a global standard in production management.

2.4. Business Model Innovation

Business model innovation redefines how a company delivers and monetizes value, often leading to new revenue streams or market expansion.

Key Characteristics:

- Changes pricing models, sales channels, or revenue structures.
- Often driven by technological advancements or market shifts.
- Can disrupt entire industries.

Example: Spotify's shift to a subscription-based model, replacing traditional music purchases with streaming services.

2.5. Technological Innovation

Technological innovation leverages emerging technologies to create new products, services, or solutions that redefine industries.

Key Characteristics:

- Driven by advances in AI, IoT, blockchain, and biotechnology.

- Often leads to radical or disruptive innovations.
- Enhances efficiency, connectivity, and automation.

Example: Cloud computing, which enabled scalable and flexible digital services, transforming software distribution (e.g., SaaS models like Microsoft 365 and Google Workspace).

2.6. Marketing Innovation

Marketing innovation introduces new ways of reaching and engaging customers, often leveraging digital transformation and data analytics.

Key Characteristics:

- Uses AI-driven personalization, influencer marketing, and interactive campaigns.
- Enhances customer engagement and brand loyalty.
- Can differentiate a brand in a competitive landscape.

Example: Nike's personalized marketing campaigns powered by AI and data analytics, creating customized experiences for customers.

2.7. Organizational Innovation

Organizational innovation improves internal structures, leadership, and workplace culture to boost efficiency and employee engagement.

Key Characteristics:

- Enhances collaboration, communication, and decision-making.
- Supports agility, creativity, and employee well-being.
- Often integrates new management frameworks.

Example: Google's 20% time policy, which allows employees to dedicate time to personal projects, fostering innovation and new ideas.

2.8. Social Innovation

Social innovation addresses societal challenges through new approaches in sustainability, education, and social equity.

Key Characteristics:

- Focuses on environmental, social, and governance (ESG) principles.
- Seeks to improve communities and global well-being.
- Often supported by government and non-profits.

Example: Microfinance initiatives, which provide small loans to entrepreneurs in developing countries, promoting financial inclusion.

2.9. Architectural Innovation

Architectural innovation reconfigures existing technology in new ways, improving overall system performance.

Key Characteristics:

- Uses known technologies in innovative combinations.
- Enhances modularity, flexibility, and efficiency.
- Bridges the gap between existing and emerging solutions.

Example: Smart home ecosystems, where IoT devices integrate to automate household functions seamlessly.

2.10. Modular Innovation

Modular innovation focuses on changing or upgrading components without altering the core structure of a product or system.

Key Characteristics:

- Maintains existing architecture but optimizes key components.
- Increases adaptability and customization.
- Supports sustainability and cost-effectiveness.

Example: Smartphones with replaceable camera modules, allowing users to upgrade specific features without replacing the entire device.

3. THE CRITICAL ROLE FOR EXECUTIVE ALIGNMENT

One of the biggest causes of failure in digital transformation is the lack of alignment at the executive level. Without strong commitment and clarity from the C-suite, digital initiatives struggle to gain traction, lose momentum, or become fragmented efforts that fail to deliver tangible business impact.

After facing numerous alignment challenges in the digital transformation programs I have led, I developed a simple but effective model to ensure true executive buy-in. This model revolves around a single principle:

3.1. Understand the Real Motivation

In my experience, C-level leaders often have hidden or unspoken reasons for wanting to innovate. These reasons range from personal career ambitions to market-driven necessities. Identifying these drivers is essential for honest, transparent alignment among executives.

Here are some real motivations I have encountered in conversations with senior leaders:

"I want to innovate to show global leadership that I deserve a promotion."

"We need to innovate to survive—our market is being disrupted."

"I want to lead the transformation of our industry before someone else does."

These motivations must be acknowledged and aligned to create a unified digital vision.

3.2. Map Common Transformation Drivers

In addition to personal motivations, companies pursue digital transformation for a variety of business-driven reasons. Below is a list of common transformation drivers that should be mapped during executive alignment discussions:

Operational Efficiency – Using automation, AI, and digital processes to reduce costs and increase productivity.

New Revenue Channels – Exploring digital products, services, or ecosystems to unlock new revenue streams.

Competitive Differentiation – Enhancing customer experience and brand positioning through digital innovation.

Market Adaptation & Survival – Responding to technological disruption and shifts in consumer behavior.

Regulatory Compliance & Risk Mitigation – Adapting to changing industry regulations and security challenges.

Scalability & Agility – Enabling organizations to adapt quickly to market fluctuations and technological advancements.

Customer-Centric Transformation – Creating hyper-personalized digital experiences to meet rising customer expectations

Sustainability & ESG Goals – Leveraging digital innovation to meet environmental, social, and governance (ESG) commitments.

To ensure strong executive buy-in, I have developed a practical framework that can be used to align CEOs, directors, and senior leaders on the digital transformation agenda. This framework helps establish a clear vision, unified objectives, and shared accountability at the leadership level.

These tools will help you build a strong digital foundation that ensures long-term transformation success.

WORKING SESSION

What is Digital Innovation for Your Company?

Identifying the role and impact of digital innovation in your company is crucial. It involves understanding how it can transform your business.

- **Ask each C-level member "What is Digital Innovation for your company?** Engaging with leadership to gather insights on digital innovation can align efforts with strategic objectives.

- **Group answers based on synergies, like the example below:**

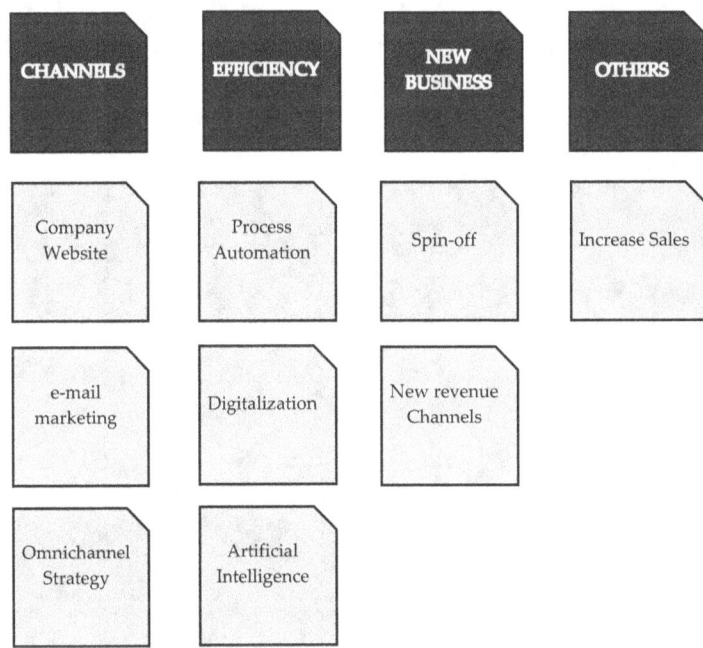

- **Reflect on Your Reasons to Innovate**: Understanding your motivations for innovation helps focus your strategy, whether for competitiveness, market entry, efficiency, or customer experience.

- **Does Any Group Combine with Your Reasons to Innovate?** Evaluating synergies between innovation types and your innovation reasons can help prioritize efforts, finding the right mix that aligns with strategic goals and market opportunities.

- **Keep this board with answers on a safe place.** We will need it when elaborating the action plan on *Chapter 4 – Action Plan*.

2. DIGITAL EVOLUTION

TLDR

This chapter content outlines the stages of digital evolution in detail, providing a clear framework for companies to assess their digital maturity and strategize their transformation journey.

ASSESSING THE DIGITAL INNOVATION MATURITY OF YOUR ORGANIZATION

1. HOW DIGITALLY ADVANCED IS YOUR SECTOR?

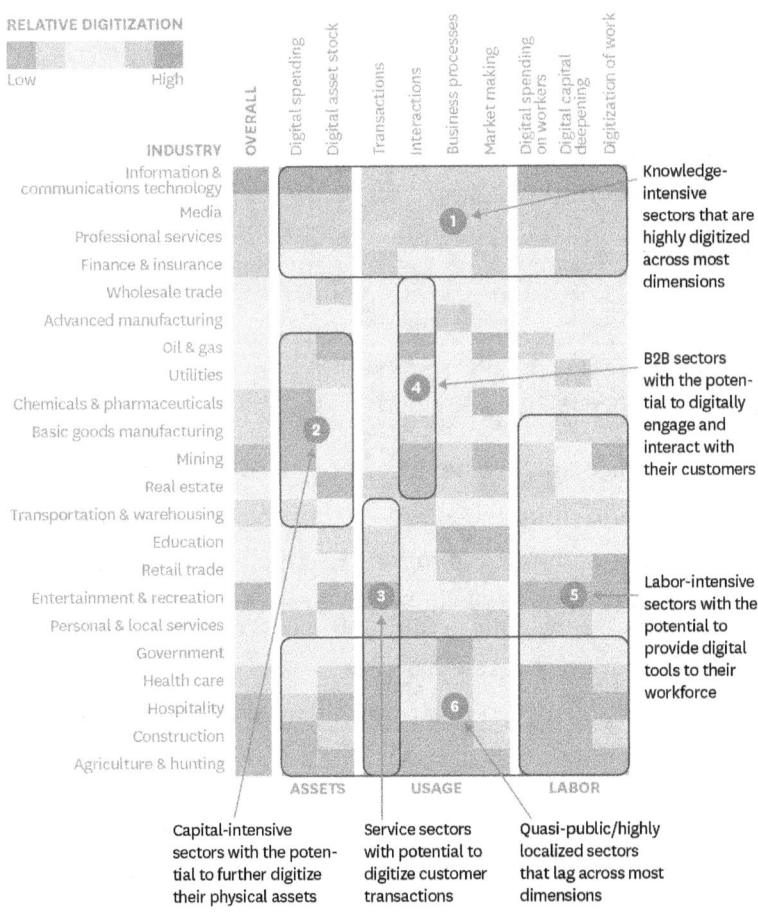

Understanding where your industry stands in the digital transformation wave is essential to positioning your business for success. Digital maturity varies significantly across sectors, with some industries pioneering digital adoption and others lagging behind. Identifying your industry's level of digitization can help you anticipate trends, identify opportunities, and develop an innovation strategy that aligns with the pace of change.

Industries can be categorized into different levels of digital advancement based on factors like digital spending, automation, data integration, and workforce digitization. The following insights can help you understand where your sector stands:

Highly Digitized Sectors (Technology, Media, Professional Services, Finance & Insurance)

These industries are at the forefront of digital transformation, leveraging automation, AI, cloud computing, and data analytics to enhance efficiency and innovation. Companies operating in these spaces must continuously evolve to maintain competitiveness.

Example: The finance sector has rapidly embraced digital banking, blockchain, and AI-driven risk assessment, shifting from traditional branch-based models to seamless digital platforms.

Capital-Intensive Industries with Digital Potential (Manufacturing, Pharmaceuticals, Oil & Gas, Utilities)

While these industries rely on large physical infrastructures, they have significant opportunities to integrate digital tools for automation, predictive maintenance, and operational efficiency.

Example: The pharmaceutical industry increasingly uses AI-driven drug discovery and digital twins to model clinical trials, accelerating the development of new treatments.

B2B Sectors Seeking Digital Engagement (Wholesale Trade, Advanced Manufacturing, Chemicals & Pharmaceuticals)

Industries serving business clients rather than consumers have the opportunity to digitally enhance interactions, streamline procurement processes, and leverage AI for supply chain optimization.

Example: Companies in wholesale trade are adopting B2B e-commerce platforms and AI-driven logistics to enhance efficiency and reduce costs.

Service Sectors with Digital Customer Potential (Retail, Hospitality, Education, Healthcare, Personal Services)

These industries benefit immensely from digital customer engagement, mobile applications, and AI-driven personalization to improve user experiences and accessibility.

Example: The rise of telemedicine in healthcare has revolutionized patient access to medical services, providing digital consultations and AI-based diagnostics.

Labor-Intensive Sectors Seeking Workforce Digitalization (Transportation, Warehousing, Construction, Agriculture)

These industries have historically been slow in digital adoption but can benefit significantly from AI-driven workforce management, IoT-enabled logistics, and automation.

Example: Smart agriculture uses IoT sensors and AI to monitor soil conditions and automate irrigation, reducing waste and increasing productivity.

Quasi-Public and Localized Sectors Lagging Behind (Government, Education, Real Estate, Entertainment & Recreation)

These sectors often experience delays in digital adoption due to regulatory constraints, outdated infrastructure, or reliance on traditional methods.

Example: Digital transformation in education has been accelerated by remote learning platforms, but many institutions still struggle with integration at scale.

2. STAGES OF DIGITAL INNOVATION MATURITY

I like to categorize the journey towards digital excellence into five distinct stages. Each stage represents a level of integration and sophistication in the use of digital technologies and strategies.

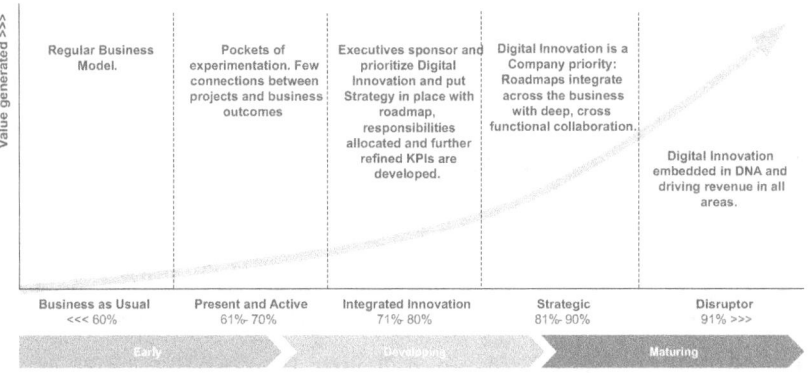

Business as Usual (< 60%): Regular Business Model

At this stage, companies operate with their traditional business models, with minimal digital integration. Digital initiatives, if any, are ad-hoc and not strategically aligned with business outcomes. The focus is on maintaining the status quo rather than seeking innovation or transformation.

Present and Active (61% - 70%): Pockets of Experimentation

Organizations begin to experiment with digital projects, but these efforts are often isolated with few connections between projects and business outcomes. There's an emerging recognition of digital's potential, but a cohesive strategy is lacking.

Integrated Innovation (71% - 80%): Strategic Digital Innovation

At this stage, executives sponsor and prioritize digital innovation. A clear strategy is in place, complete with a roadmap, allocated responsibilities, and refined KPIs. Digital projects are more connected, and there's a concerted effort to align them with the company's broader goals.

Strategic (81% - 90%): Company-Wide Priority

Digital innovation becomes a company-wide priority. Roadmaps for digital projects are integrated across the business, fostering deep, cross-functional collaboration. The organization begins to break down silos, encouraging a culture of innovation and agility.

Disruptor (>91%): Embedded Digital Innovation

In the final stage of digital maturity, digital innovation is embedded in the organization's DNA. It drives revenue in all areas, with the company often setting new standards in its industry. These organizations are seen as disruptors, leading the way with new business models and groundbreaking technologies.

WORKING SESSION

The Digital Innovation Maturity Assessment

The next step is to look at your organization and identify which stage of digital maturity it is on. This is not an exercise in judgment, but one of self-awareness. Your current position on the scale does not determine your value but provides a starting point for your digital transformation journey.

Self-assessment: After reading each pair of statements, reflect on the current situation of your company on the topic in question. Then, choose the number, on the scale of 1 to 7, which best indicates where your organization is in relation to the 2 statements: 1 indicates fully compatible with the information on the left, 7 indicates totally compatible with the situation on the right.

<<<<<<<<<<<<<<<<<<<<	1	2	3	4	5	6	7	>>>>>>>>>>>>>>>>>>>>
We are focused on selling and interacting with our customers through the usual channels.								We are focused on the continuous change of digital habits and the customer's shopping journeys.
We use marketing to target, reach and persuade customers.								We use marketing to attract, engage, inspire, and collaborate with our customers.
Our brand and reputation are what we communicate to our customers.								The support and promotion of our customers are the best reference on our brand and reputation.

Our exclusive competitive focus is to outdo our competitors.						We are open to collaborating with our competitors and competing with our partners.
We seek to create value exclusively through our products.						We seek to create value through external platforms and networks.
We are mainly focused on our own sector and our direct competitors.						We face competition as a process beyond our own industry.
Our data strategy is focused on how to create, store, and manage our data.						Our data strategy is focused on how to convert the data to a new value.
We use our data to manage the day-to-day operations.						We manage our data as strategic assets that we are building over time.
Our data is in the division or business unit where it was generated.						Our data is organized to be accessible by all divisions of the company.
We take decisions based on analysis, debates, and hierarchical level.						We take decisions based on experiments and tests, whenever possible.
Our innovation projects always exceed deadlines and funds.						We innovate in short cycles, using prototypes to learn quickly.
We try to avoid failure in new ventures at all costs.						We accept failure in new ventures, but we seek to reduce costs and increase learning.
Our value proposition is defined by our products and our industry						Our value proposition is defined by the changing needs of customers.
We evaluate new technologies by the way they impact our current businesses.						We evaluate new technologies by how they can create new value for our customers.
We are focused on executing and optimizing our current business model.						Our aim is to adapt early to stay ahead of the change curve.
Our IT investments are considered operational investments.						Our IT investments are considered strategic.

INNOVATION WITHOUT DRAMA

It is difficult to allocate resources outside current lines of business.						We can invest in new ventures, even if they compete with our ongoing businesses.
Our main performance metrics relate only to sustaining ongoing businesses.						Our business metrics are adapted to be compatible with the strategy and maturity of a line of business.
Managers are responsible and rewarded for immediate results in achieving past goals.						Managers are responsible and rewarded based on long-term goals and new strategies.
We have difficulties in developing new ventures away from ongoing businesses						We can build and cultivate new ideas that are unusual for our ongoing businesses.
Sharing best practices across the organization is slow and inconsistent.						We can take advantage of successful new ideas and integrate them across the organization.
Our highest priority is to maximize return for shareholders.						Our highest priority is to create value for our shareholders.
Traditional HR functions focus on managing talent operations. They do not receive help from digital, they are not a motivator for digital change, nor are they in the position to lead the transformation.						HR is a leadership partner in the definition and implementation of Digital Transformation. HR is provocative because it takes risks, tries new approaches and goes beyond the company, in a broader HR community.
The company has good internal control systems, but they do not "talk" with the systems of suppliers, customers, and business partners.						The company uses digital platforms to collaborate and share data with its main suppliers and business partners.
The company has indicators and a system for managing process results, productivity, quality, and customer satisfaction.						The company measures the benefits of the initiatives through new indicators (OKRs), inspiring collaboration and boosting efforts.
The company has a clear strategy and a long-term view of the current business. It has the plan broken down into actions and uses indicators to monitor the implementation of its strategy.						There is a clear vision of what the company wants (purpose), which is permeated by the organization and its business partners, being receptive to adjust its long-term plans

The company uses systems such as CRM and ERP. It also seeks, through process improvement techniques (Lean, Kaisen, TPM, etc.) to increase its productivity and reduce costs to always remain competitive.						For business functions (marketing and sales, finance, product manufacturing and distribution, procurement, HR, and talent acquisition / retention), the company uses technologies such as cloud, mobility, and Artificial Intelligence to improve operational efficiency.
We have an efficient communication system, through our websites and social media. Our marketing investment is directed to newspapers, magazines, and television.						Our customers can use any means of interacting with our company in a fluid and agile way. Our website is responsive, that is, s and automatically adapts to the screen size of the device the customer is using.
I'm interested in the topic, but I still can't understand how Digital Innovation will affect my careers, work, and business.						I have a full understanding of Digital Innovation and I have an idea of how it will impact my career, my work, and the business.

FINAL SCORE

The maximum score is 203 points. Add your result and divide by 203. Multiply per 100 and get *Your Organization Score.*

([   ] / 203) x 100 = [   ] %

    TOTAL SCORE   YOUR ORGANIZATION SCORE

Now, based on your organization score percentage, check in which stage of the digital innovation evolution is your organization:

INNOVATION WITHOUT DRAMA

Value generated >>>

Business as Usual (<<< 60%) — *Early*	Regular Business Model.
Present and Active (61%–70%) — *Early*	Pockets of experimentation. Few connections between projects and business outcomes
Integrated Innovation (71%–80%) — *Developing*	Executives sponsor and prioritize Digital Innovation and put Strategy in place with roadmap, responsibilities allocated and further refined KPIs are developed.
Strategic (81%–90%) — *Developing / Maturing*	Digital Innovation is a Company priority: Roadmaps integrate across the business with deep, cross functional collaboration.
Disruptor (91% >>>) — *Maturing*	Digital Innovation embedded in DNA and driving revenue in all areas.

Inspired on: Framework by Altimeter - The Race Against Digital Darwinism: six stages of digital transformation & The Digital Transformation Journey - Luis Lobão and Carlos Zilli

If you are implementing new strategies to enhance your organization's Digital Innovation Maturity score, it is advisable to conduct a fresh assessment next year and compare the results.

---

3. DIGITAL AMBITION

TLDR

This chapter explores the strategic considerations and organizational structures essential for successful digital transformation. It balances optimizing existing processes with creating new business models and examines the placement and role of digital innovation within organizations. Additionally, it provides practical guidance on defining an aspirational purpose for digital initiatives and crafting a powerful digital statement, helping you articulate your digital ambition effectively.

DEFINING YOUR ORGANIZATION'S DIGITAL FUTURE

In this chapter, we delve into the strategic considerations and organizational structures that underpin successful digital transformation. We explore the balance between optimizing existing processes and creating new business models, the placement and role of digital innovation within the organization, and how leading companies like Apple structure themselves to foster innovation. Additionally, we provide guidance on defining a purposeful and aspirational statement for digital initiatives, offering practical tools and templates to help you articulate your digital ambition effectively.

A company's digital ambition should be more than just a collection of projects. It must be a bold, actionable vision that unites leadership, aligns teams, and sets the direction for innovation.

1. BALANCE OPTIMIZATION VS NEW BUSINESS

A common mistake companies make is failing to define the scope of their digital ambition. For some, digital transformation means optimizing internal processes (efficiency-driven). For others, it means creating entirely new business models (growth-driven).

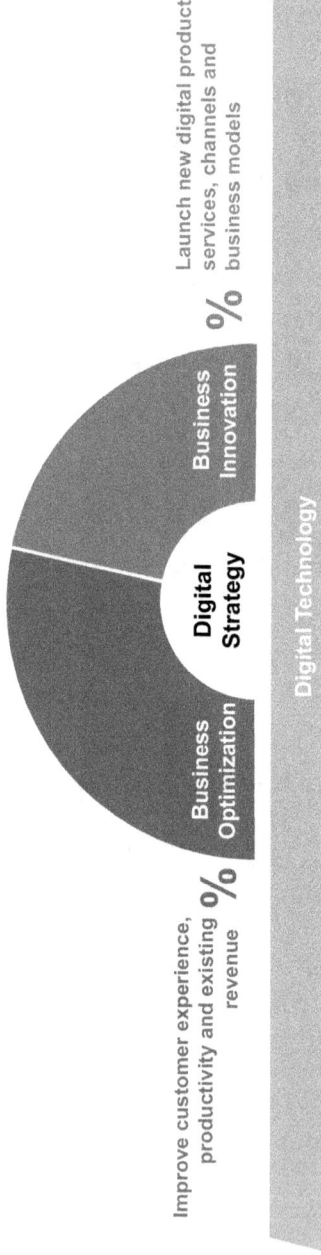

Business Optimization

Automating manual workflows, reducing costs, and improving speed.

Example: Implementing AI-driven logistics for real-time tracking and faster deliveries.

Business Innovation

Launching new digital products, services, or revenue streams.

Example: A traditional car dealership expanding into digital insurance and online vehicle leasing.

The key to success is balance and clarity — understanding whether digital ambition is primarily about improving existing operations or reinventing the business model entirely.

2. DEFINE AN ASPIRATIONAL PURPOSE

Setting a clear and aspirational purpose for your digital innovation efforts is essential. This purpose should align with your overall business strategy (C-level alignment), reflect your current position in the journey (Digital Maturity Score), represents the balance between business optimization and business innovation) and define where you want to be serving as a guide and an inspiration.

At the end of this chapter, you will find a toolkit to help you navigate this process and craft a strong statement that truly reflects your digital innovation ambition.

3. UNDERSTAND THE ORGANIZATIONAL STRUCTURE

Different companies require different organizational structures to support their digital ambition. Apple, for example, uses a functional organization, where teams are structured by expertise rather than product lines. This contrasts with traditional business-unit structures, where teams operate independently.

Key Considerations:

- Should digital innovation be centralized (with a dedicated digital unit) or decentralized (integrated into business units)?
- Does the company require cross-functional teams to break down silos and improve agility?
- Should digital projects be spun off into separate ventures to accelerate speed and autonomy?

3.1. Where Should I Put the Digital Innovation Area?

Many large corporations struggle with digital transformation because they try to force innovation within rigid, traditional structures. Sometimes, the best approach is to create independent teams, new business units, or even spin-offs to drive digital ambition forward.

Up next, you will find the complete framework I use to determine where the Digital Innovation function should be positioned within the organization and how it aligns with the company's understanding of Digital Innovation — an understanding you defined in the workshop introduced in *Chapter 1, Your Reason to Innovate*. This framework includes pros and cons of each model and how they fit on the current digital innovation maturity.

Organizational Design

Decentralized
Digital is low priority

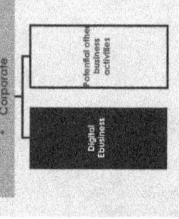

- Each BU manages digital strategy and delivery independently with little exchange

+ Very close to BU & function needs
+ Suitable when small digital business impact
- Limited re-use / scale
- Low flexibility / long cycles
- IT costs can explode.

Shared services
Digital is important

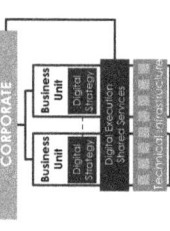

- BU manages digital business and priorities
- Centralized shared services for execution (it-driven and output focused)

+ Scale & agility effects for digital infrastructure
+ Strategy is close to BU
+ Cost efficiencies
- Split accountability
- Relies on business / IT collaboration

Center of Excellence
Digital is major priority

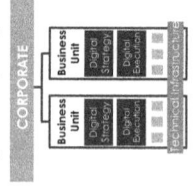

- CoE provides expertise, rules & supports strategy
- In cases, coe and shared services (execution) can be integrated into one entity

+ Central access to digital skills / delivery combined with close business link
+ Digital consistency
- Dual reporting, may lead to limited BU control
- Requires heavy governance

Centralized
Digital is core to the business

- Single centralized unit
- Unit may reside in other function e.g. Marketing.

+ Digital growth / innovation
+ Effective skill allocation
+ Full integration across bus and central entity
- Potential disconnect with smaller BU or local needs & priorities

Spin-off / digital-only
Digital is the business

- Separate entity focused on digital only
- Ecommerce business

+ Complete focus on digital
+ Scale / agility / skills
- In case of other activities, potential conflict of positioning

→ Digital maturity increase →

3.2. What We Can Learn From Apple's Organizational Structure

- **The Functional Structure**

    In 1997, Steve Jobs revolutionized Apple's organizational structure, moving away from traditional business units to a functional model. This shift ensured that experts in specific domains, rather than general managers, held decision-making authority. This commitment to a functional structure has been a cornerstone of Apple's ability to thrive in a dynamic & evolving innovation landscape.

    Inspirational leadership: Each VP is an expert on its nitch, driving the vision of that specific function and inspiring the team.

    Autonomy to make intuitive decisions: Innovation is not about asking customers what they want. Innovation is based on the judgment and intuition of technical experts. In this model, experts are more likely to be right about customer needs than general managers or even traditional focus groups.

    Easier Budgeting cycle: There is only one P&L, so there is no fight for the budget on the product level. It is a top-down decision on where to put the money.

- **The leadership model**

    Experts leading experts:

    Apple prioritizes expertise, believing that it is easier to train an expert to manage effectively than to train a manager to become an expert.

    Immersion in the details:

    Leaders are expected to immerse themselves in their organization, understanding issues at least three levels down. This hands-on approach ensures a deep understanding of the details.

    Willingness to collaboratively debate:

    Apple fosters a culture of collaborative debate, encouraging leaders to engage in discussions that involve diverse perspectives. This approach is integral to the decision-making process, ensuring thorough vetting of ideas and perspectives.

- **Leadership at scale**

    As Apple has grown from 8,000 (in 1998) to 137,000 employees (in 2019), the functional structure has faced challenges. Leaders have had to balance their deep expertise with the necessity of delegation.

The adaptability of Apple's leadership within a functional organization is evident, showcasing the company's ability to evolve with extraordinary growth.

WORKING SESSION

How to Write a Powerful Digital Innovation Statement That Resonates?

Crafting a compelling digital innovation statement is an art. It should encapsulate your digital ambition, resonate with stakeholders, and inspire action. This section offers practical tips on creating a statement that captures the essence of your digital vision.

Golden Circle Template

Simon Sinek's Golden Circle framework is an invaluable tool for articulating your digital ambition. By focusing on the 'why,' 'how,' and 'what' of your digital initiatives, you can create a clear and compelling narrative that drives engagement and alignment across your organization.

- Do keep it short and concise. Sum up the digital innovation ambition in just a few sentences.

- Don't write an essay. That is not the purpose of this tool. You want the digital innovation ambition to be tethered to the brand and that means it must be memorable. Long drawn out prose is rarely memorable.

- Do think long-term. The ambition is an investment in your company's future, so keep it open enough to reflect your long-term goals.

- Don't make it too limiting. We want to provide the best products ever to the town of Elmwood. Do you only see the business selling to the residents of one small town or do you hope to expand at some point?

- Do find out what your employees think of the digital innovation ambition. This is a tool designed with them in mind, too, so get their opinion. Ask how they would improve it and what they dislike about it.

- Don't be afraid to change it. Things change in the business world. If the digital innovation ambition no longer represents the company's vision, it is time for a rewrite.

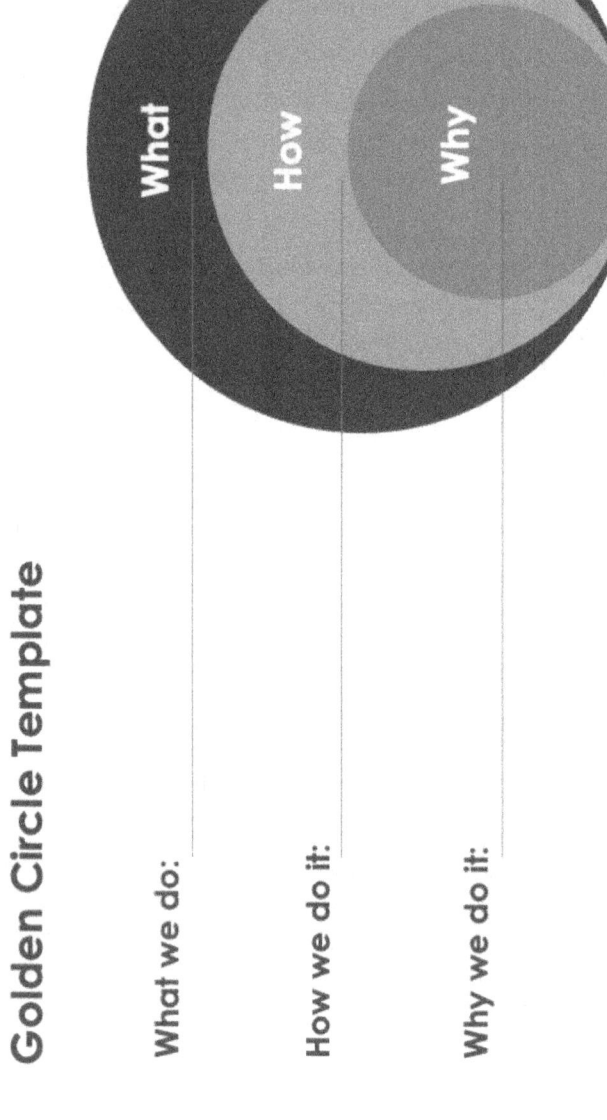

Golden Circle Template

What we do: _____

How we do it: _____

Why we do it: _____

4. ACTION PLAN

TLDR

In this chapter, I guide you through the initial steps of our innovation journey, beginning with identifying customer pain points, setting up pilot projects and securing quick wins, and exploring various innovation models.

FROM VISION TO ACTION

Innovation is not about brainstorming in a closed room, dreaming of the next billion-dollar idea. It's about execution. Structured, iterative, and outcome-driven. A great vision without a concrete action plan is just wishful thinking.

Through my journey, whether building startups from scratch or driving transformation in S&P 500 companies, I learned that turning ideas into reality follows a repeatable process. You don't need a blank check or unlimited time. What you need is a systematic approach that aligns leadership, teams, and execution frameworks toward clear, measurable outcomes.

In this chapter, I will walk you through the key steps to creating an Action Plan that drives results while avoiding the common pitfalls that prevent innovation from scaling.

1. START BY MAPPING CUSTOMER'S PAIN POINTS

If you want to create meaningful impact, don't start with a solution—start with a problem. The most successful innovation efforts are born from a deep understanding of customer pain points.

Talk to real customers. Go beyond surveys and NPS scores. Have conversations. Observe their behavior.

Find patterns. The best insights often come from spotting unmet needs across different segments.

Validate quickly. Before jumping into full execution, ensure there is a real need for what you're building.

A simple but effective exercise is to map the customer journey and identify friction points where users struggle. These are your opportunities for innovation.

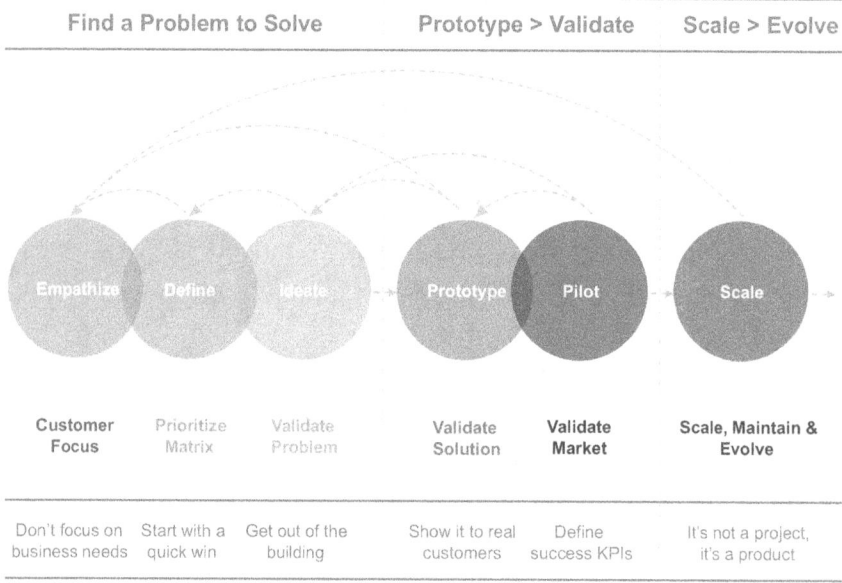

2. UNDERSTAND THE DIFFERENT INNOVATION MODELS

Everyone talks about Innovation, but today, we're breaking it down for you in an easy and valuable way. We delve into diverse innovation models that can reshape the way organizations thrive.

Each model holds strategic significance, and the real magic happens when we combine them.

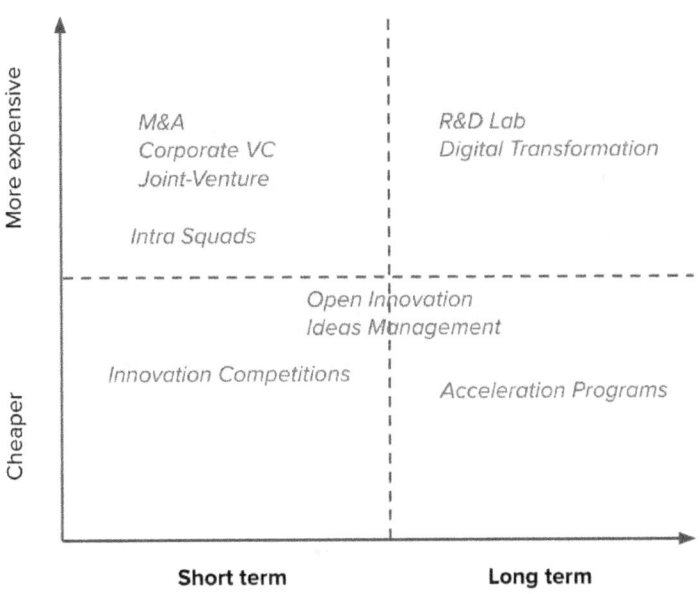

2.1. Merger and Acquisitions (M&A)

M&A involves one company acquiring another, typically for strategic reasons such as entering new markets, gaining a competitive edge, or obtaining valuable assets.

Use Case: When a technology company acquires a startup with cutting-edge software to enhance its product portfolio and stay ahead of the competition.

Pros:

- Rapid entry into new markets

- Access to established customer bases
- Synergies in combining resources and capabilities

Cons:

- Integration challenges and cultural clashes
- Regulatory hurdles
- High upfront costs

2.2. Corporate Venture Capital

Corporate VC is when a large corporation invests in external startups to gain strategic advantages, foster innovation, and potentially realize financial returns.

Use Case: An established automotive company investing in a promising electric vehicle startup to stay at the forefront of the evolving transportation industry.

Pros:

- Access to external innovation and startups
- Potential for high returns on successful investments
- Opportunities for strategic partnerships

Cons:

- Risk of startup failures impacting returns
- Potential conflicts of interest
- Resource-intensive to manage

2.3. Joint-Venture

A joint venture is a collaboration between two or more companies to pursue a specific project or business opportunity, sharing risks and rewards.

Use Case: Two pharmaceutical companies forming a joint venture to develop and commercialize a groundbreaking medical treatment.

Pros:

- Shared risks and resources
- Access to partner's expertise and market knowledge
- Faster market entry with a local partner

Cons:

- Shared decision-making can be complex
- Potential for conflicts between partners
- Limited control over the venture

2.4. Innovation Competitions

Organizations organize competitions to source innovative ideas externally or internally, encouraging participants to compete for rewards or recognition.

Use Case: A technology company hosting a hackathon to gather creative solutions for enhancing its software development processes.

Pros:

- Encourages creativity and diverse solutions
- Identifies talent within and outside the organization
- Generates a buzz around innovation

Cons:

- May result in many ideas without implementation
- Potential bias in judging
- Limited to the ideas submitted

2.5. R&D Lab

Research and Development Labs are internal units dedicated to exploring new technologies, conducting experiments, and developing innovative solutions.

Use Case: A consumer electronics company establishing an R&D lab to pioneer advancements in wearable technology.

Pros:

- Focused on long-term technological advancements
- Intellectual property development
- Nurtures a culture of research and development

Cons:

- High costs with uncertain returns
- Long gestation periods for tangible outcomes
- May face challenges in aligning with business objectives

2.6. Acceleration Programs

Acceleration programs support startups or intrapreneurs by providing mentorship, resources, and funding to rapidly develop and scale their ideas.

Use Case: An innovation hub running an acceleration program for startups focused on sustainable energy solutions.

Pros:

- Rapid development and growth of startups
- Access to mentorship and resources
- Potential for disruptive innovation

Cons:

- High failure rate among startups
- Limited scalability of successful startups
- Resource-intensive to manage

2.7. Intrapreneurship Squads

Intrapreneurship involves employees within a company taking on entrepreneurial roles to drive innovation from within.

Use Case: A large retail corporation creating intrapreneurship squads to explore and implement new technologies for improving the customer shopping experience.

Pros:

- Harnesses internal talent and creativity
- Encourages a culture of innovation within the organization
- Taps into employees' knowledge of the company

Cons:

- May face resistance from traditional structures
- Resource allocation challenges
- Success depends on the entrepreneurial spirit of employees

2.8. Ideas Management

This involves systematically collecting, evaluating, and implementing ideas from employees or external stakeholders to drive innovation.

Use Case: A manufacturing company implementing an ideas management platform to gather suggestions from employees on process improvements and cost-saving measures.

Pros:

- Involves employees in the innovation process
- Diverse input from various levels of the organization
- Fosters a culture of continuous improvement

Cons:

- Overwhelming volume of ideas to manage
- Implementation challenges for all suggested ideas
- Potential for duplication of efforts

2.9. Open Innovation

Open Innovation involves collaborating with external partners, such as suppliers, customers, or other organizations, to jointly develop and implement innovative solutions.

Use Case: A beverage company collaborating with a packaging supplier to develop sustainable and eco-friendly packaging solutions.

Pros:

- Access to external expertise and ideas
- Expands the innovation ecosystem
- Collaborative problem-solving

Cons:

- Requires effective management of external partnerships
- Potential intellectual property concerns
- Challenges in aligning external ideas with internal strategies

2.10. Digital Transformation

Digital Transformation is a comprehensive organizational change leveraging digital technologies to improve business processes, customer experiences, and overall efficiency.

Use Case: A traditional banking institution undergoing digital transformation to shift from brick-and-mortar operations to a seamless online banking experience.

Pros:

- Enhances operational efficiency
- Improves customer experiences
- Positions the company for future growth

Cons:

- Resistance to change from employees
- High initial costs of technology adoption
- Continuous need for updates and adaptation

3. DEFINE PILOTS & QUICK WINS

By defining pilots and focusing on quick wins, organizations can test ideas in the real world, gathering invaluable feedback without the need for massive upfront investment. These small victories not only validate concepts but also build confidence and support for broader initiatives.

- Focus on two or three flagship initiatives
- Run collaborative experiments and then scale what works
- Develop organization for new business models

3.1. Revisit Your Reason to Innovate

Now is the time to revisit the workshop outcome from *Chapter 1 – Your Reason to Innovate*, where you defined your reason for innovation and gathered insights from C-level leadership on what digital innovation truly means for your company. This step is crucial to ensuring alignment and strategic coherence as you define your pilots.

3.2. Select the Right Initiatives

- Identify two or three initiatives that align with your customers' pain points, introduced in this chapter, and combine them with your core reason for innovation. These initiatives must be relevant to your industry's level of digital maturity (a concept I introduced in *Chapter 2 – Digital Evolution*).

- Ensure these initiatives align with your company's digital innovation maturity score to avoid launching projects that are either too advanced or too basic for your organization's current state. You can find your score in the Working Session of *Chapter 2 – Digital Evolution*.

- Validate that these initiatives align with the Digital Innovation Ambition you crafted in *Chapter 3 – Digital*

Ambition to ensure they contribute to your broader strategic vision.

- Check which Innovation Model, introduced in this chapter, aligns best to deliver the two or three initiatives.

3.3. Structure It for Success

Once you have identified the right initiatives, revisit your organizational design, a concept I introduced in *Chapter 3 - Digital Ambition*, to determine where they fit best within your company's structure. Consider the most effective model for assembling the team that will execute these initiatives.

WORKING SESSION

Prioritization Tools to Focus on What Really Matters

To help you prioritize and select the most strategic flagship initiatives, I introduce simple yet powerful prioritization tools. These will help you narrow your focus to the most impactful opportunities, setting you up for a successful execution phase.

Value vs Complexity | Effort

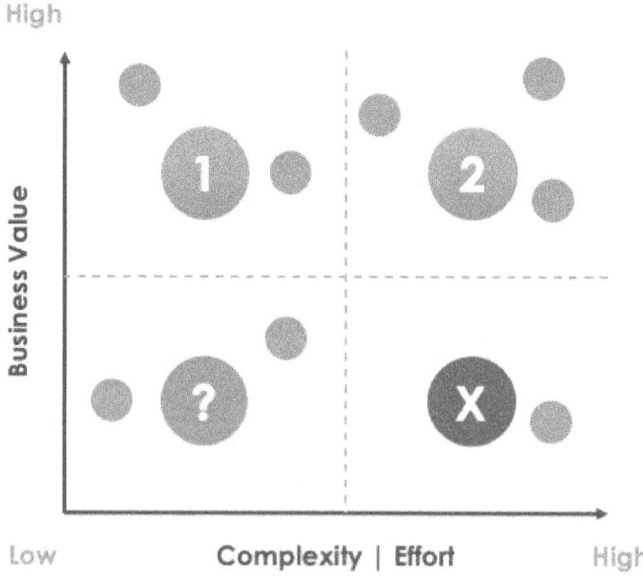

When selecting your flagship initiatives, balancing potential value with implementation complexity is crucial. The Value vs Complexity (or Effort) Matrix helps prioritize projects by weighing their expected impact against the effort required to execute them. This method ensures you focus on initiatives that deliver high value with manageable complexity.

Kano Model

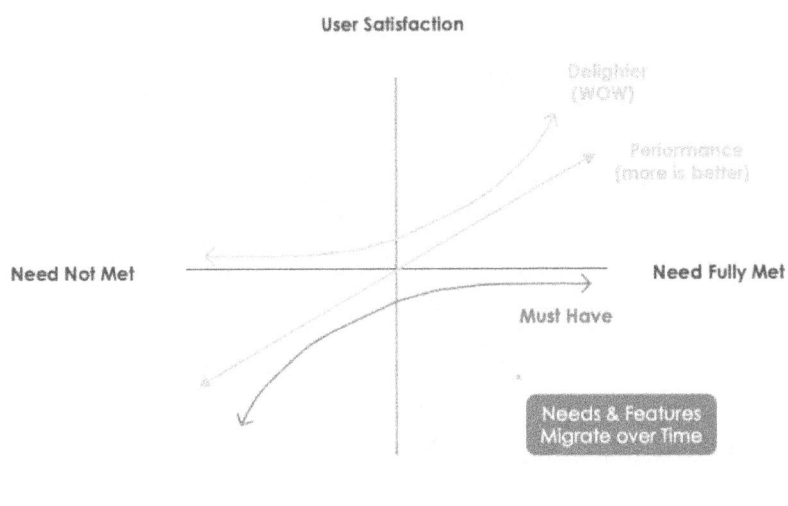

Not all innovations generate the same level of customer satisfaction. The Kano Model helps categorize initiatives based on how they influence customer delight, from basic must-haves to game-changing differentiators. This framework is essential for prioritizing innovations that truly resonate with users.

MoSCoW Method

Prioritization often requires distinguishing between what's essential and what can wait. The MoSCoW Method (Must-have, Should-have, Could-have, and Won't-have) provides a structured approach to identifying the critical features and projects that should take precedence.

RICE Scoring Model

For data-driven decision-making, the RICE Scoring Model (Reach, Impact, Confidence, Effort) provides a quantitative way to prioritize initiatives. By assigning scores across these dimensions, you can objectively assess which projects are most likely to drive meaningful results.

5. EXECUTION

TLDR

This chapter shows how to turn your innovation strategy into action. You'll learn how to build empowered squads, apply agile methods, and embrace moonshot thinking to drive bold results. Key mindset shifts — from projects to products, from building to last to building to change, and from big-bang launches to baby steps — will help your organization adapt faster. You'll also explore how to align Digital, IT, and Business teams, define quick-win pilots, and use OKRs to measure success. Plus, you'll gain tools like growth funnels, Design Jams, and MVPs to accelerate innovation with real impact.

EXECUTING DIGITAL INNOVATION

In this chapter, I delve into the essence of executing digital innovation within your organization. It's a journey that transcends traditional boundaries, embracing a future where technology and human ingenuity intersect to create value. As we navigate through this chapter, we'll explore the critical components that make up the backbone of digital innovation.

1. BRING YOUR HEROES

No breakthrough happens in isolation — especially not inside the walls of a large corporation. When it comes to executing digital innovation, you're not just building something new; you're going up against an entire operating system built to preserve the status quo.

Big companies have strong immune systems. They're engineered for efficiency, predictability, and risk mitigation. Their structures, governance models, and incentive systems were designed to protect what already exists — not to welcome what's new or uncertain. Innovation, in this context, isn't just hard — it's often actively repelled. That's why you can't rely on ordinary teams or junior talent to lead this charge.

You'll need heroes.

These are your boldest thinkers, most curious doers, and sharpest executors. People who not only understand how to navigate corporate complexity, but who also have the courage and creativity to challenge it. You're looking for individuals who are driven by purpose, not protocol — and who are comfortable being uncomfortable. In most cases, you'll only get one shot to prove that digital innovation isn't just theater — it can move the needle in real business results.

I've seen this firsthand. When I've staffed my innovation teams, I've intentionally brought in former entrepreneurs, ex-startup leaders, and high performers from adjacent industries. These professionals are naturally resourceful, adaptive, and hungry for impact. They're not conditioned to ask for permission; they figure things out, test fast, and push forward. They know how to get results without a manual.

Most importantly, your heroes must be aligned by a shared mission and a bias for action. Innovation doesn't come from assembling a group of generalists and hoping magic happens. It comes from deliberately curating a strike team with complementary skills, shared trust, and a burning desire to build what's next — even when the system fights back.

You're not staffing a project. You're building a resistance against inertia.

So ask yourself:

Who are the three to five people in your organization (or outside of it) that you'd bet on to deliver the impossible?

Those are your heroes. Bring them in early. Empower them fully. And give them a challenge worthy of their ambition.

1.1. Identify Internal Talent with a Growth Mindset

Start by scanning your organization for hidden gems — intrapreneurs, digital champions, or people who consistently challenge the status quo.

Look for those who are curious, fast learners, and respected by peers — not just for their technical skills, but for their adaptability and problem-solving.

1.2. Blend with External Experts

Internal talent alone may not be enough. Bring in outsiders with fresh perspectives, preferably from startups, scale-ups, or other digitally advanced organizations.

These people bring the speed, creativity, and mindset that large corporations often lack — and they raise the bar for the rest of the team.

1.3. Mix Industry Expertise

Don't just look within your own sector. Some of the most powerful innovation comes from cross-industry thinking.

Refer to the table "How Digitally Advanced is Your Sector?" in Chapter 2 – Digital Evolution.

Target talent from industries like fintech, retail, gaming, or healthtech — areas that are typically ahead in digital transformation.

1.4. Partner with a Forward-Thinking Talent Acquisition Team

Your HR or talent acquisition team must be part of the mission. Share your digital vision and make sure they understand you're hiring for a mission, not just a role.

Co-create JD templates that are aspirational, inspiring, and challenge-driven — not your usual list of job requirements and perks.

1.5. Sell the Vision, Not Just the Role

Top talent is not moved by salary alone. They want to be part of something meaningful.

Share the compelling Digital Ambition you developed in Chapter 3. Show them how their work will impact the business, the customer, and the industry.

Use storytelling — people join movements, not PowerPoints.

1.6. Be Aspirational in Job Descriptions

Write JD's like you're building the next SpaceX. Use ambitious, purpose-driven language.

Frame the role as a rare opportunity to make history inside a big company — to challenge norms, to change lives, to lead a movement.

1.7. Pay Well — They're Heroes, Not Replacements

You're not hiring to fill gaps. You're hiring heroes to move mountains. Compensate accordingly.

Consider incentive structures, equity-like bonuses, or innovation-linked KPIs. Think beyond HR policy.

1.8. Protect the Heroes

Give them room to breathe. Remove unnecessary governance and slow approval layers.

Shield them from corporate inertia — create an environment where it's okay to test, fail, learn, and try again.

1.9. Reignite Their Fire Regularly

Regularly connect their work back to the vision. Remind them that they are changing the company, one sprint at a time.

Celebrate small wins loudly. Let the rest of the company see what's possible when the right people are given the right mission.

2. ORGANIZE THEM INTO SQUADS

Inspired by the Spotify model, high-performing organizations move away from rigid, siloed structures and embrace agile squads — small, empowered teams with clear ownership.

I typically have these areas and talents.

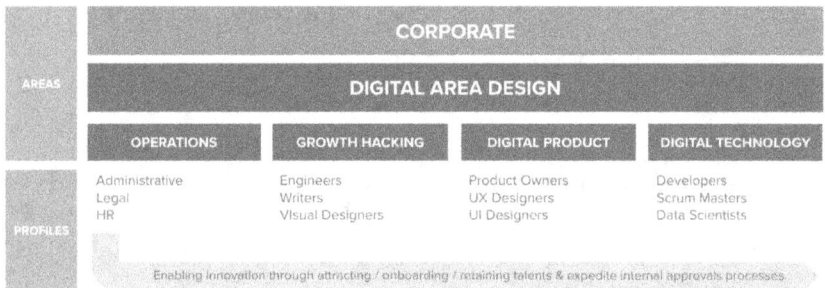

Then break down silos and organize your heroes into agile squads — Think of these squads as small startup-like groups within the company.

A squad operates under a unique framework that emphasizes autonomy, cross-functionality, and a strong focus on end-to-end responsibility. Here's a breakdown of how a squad works within Spotify's agile engineering culture:

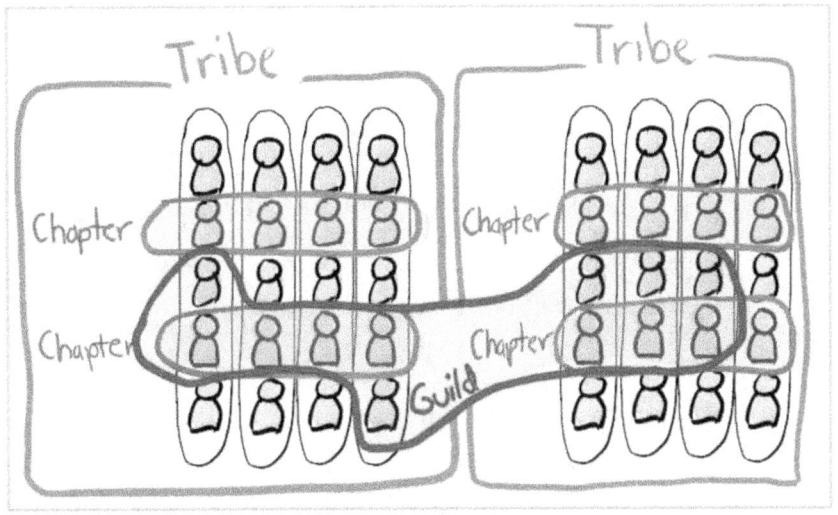

2.1. Squad Definition and Structure

Autonomous Unit: A squad is a small, self-organizing team, typically comprising fewer than eight members. It functions autonomously within the broader organizational framework of Spotify, making decisions on what to build, how to build it, and how to collaborate during the process.

Cross-functional Composition: Squads are cross-functional, meaning they include members with all the skills and expertise necessary to take a product or feature from concept to deployment. This includes design, development, testing, and operations.

End-to-End Responsibility: Each squad has end-to-end responsibility for the products or features they work on. This encompasses design, development, deployment, maintenance, and operations, ensuring a holistic approach to product development and maintenance.

2.2. Operating Principles

Autonomy with Boundaries: While squads have the autonomy to decide on their work, this freedom comes with boundaries. They must align their decisions with the squad's mission, the overall product strategy, and the company's goals. They're also expected to renegotiate short-term goals every quarter to stay aligned with the company's objectives.

Collaborative Environment: Spotify's office layout is optimized for squad collaboration. Squad areas are designed to facilitate easy access among team members, with adjustable desks, lounge areas for group discussions, and quiet rooms for focused work or smaller meetings. Almost all walls are whiteboards, encouraging spontaneous brainstorming and problem-solving.

Culture of Trust and Respect: The success of the squad model relies heavily on a culture of mutual respect and trust. Members are encouraged to give credit to each other, and there's a notable absence of ego despite the high talent density. This environment fosters open communication and collaboration, essential for the autonomous yet aligned functioning of squads.

2.3. Goals and Alignment

Mission-Driven: Each squad has a long-term mission that guides its projects and initiatives. This mission-driven approach ensures that the squad's work contributes meaningfully to Spotify's overall objectives and product strategy.

Loosely Coupled but Tightly Aligned: Squads operate under the principle of being loosely coupled but tightly aligned. This means they work independently but are closely aligned with Spotify's goals, product strategy, and other squads. The aim is to create synergy within the Spotify ecosystem, where squads complement each other's work without unnecessary dependencies or coordination.

2.4. Continuous Improvement

Experimentation and Learning: Squads are encouraged to experiment and learn from both successes and failures. This iterative approach allows squads to continuously improve their processes, products, and collaboration methods.

Feedback and Adaptation: Regular planning sessions, retrospectives, and the use of metrics for decision-making help squads adapt and evolve their strategies based on feedback and performance data.

3. FOLLOW THE 2 PIZZA RULE

When it comes to executing innovation, team size matters more than you think.

According to Hackman's Law, the number of communication links between team members increases exponentially with team size. The formula is:

Communication Links = N * (N - 1) / 2

Where N is the number of people in the team.

For example:

A team of 5 has 10 links to manage.

A team of 10 has 45.

A team of 20 has 190.

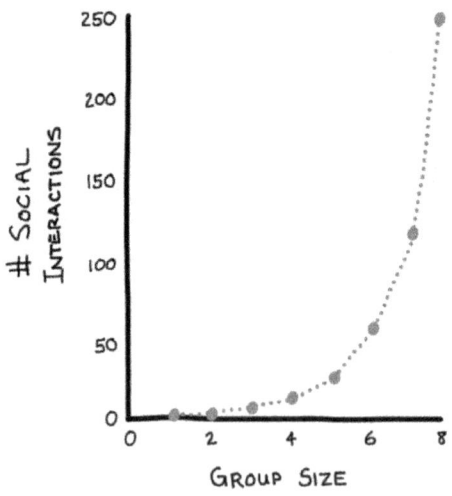

The more links, the more overhead, misalignment, and delays. Suddenly, the team spends more time aligning with each other than executing the work.

That's why Jeff Bezos famously introduced the Two-Pizza Rule at Amazon:

"If a team can't be fed with two pizzas, it's too big."

That usually translates to 5–7 people. Small enough to stay nimble, fast, and autonomous.

3.1. Why Smaller Teams Drive Better Innovation

- **Faster Decision-Making**

    With fewer people in the room, decisions are made quickly. There's less waiting, less ping-ponging of emails, and less "meetings about meetings."

- **Higher Ownership & Accountability**

    In smaller teams, every member is critical. People naturally take more responsibility, own their outcomes, and feel more connected to the mission.

- **Better Focus & Clarity**

    Small teams are easier to align around a single goal. You don't need layers of documentation to explain the "why." Everyone is on the same page.

- **Stronger Culture & Trust**

    Psychological safety grows faster in tight-knit groups. People are more willing to share bold ideas, take risks, and experiment — critical for innovation.

- **Reduced Complexity**

    Fewer people = fewer dependencies = fewer delays. It becomes easier to ship fast, test early, and adapt.

3.2. Amazon's Example

At Amazon, the Two-Pizza Rule isn't just a fun metaphor — it's a core principle behind how they structure innovation teams.

Each product or initiative is assigned to a "two-pizza team".

These teams operate like internal startups, with autonomy, their own metrics, and the freedom to ship independently.

Many of Amazon's groundbreaking innovations — like Prime, AWS, and Kindle — came from small, focused teams that could move faster than the rest of the org.

By keeping teams small and nimble, Amazon avoids the bureaucratic drag that slows down most large organizations.

Time for Some Math

Do the math:

How many people do you currently engage with on a traditional project in your company?

Now calculate how many communication links that creates using:

$$N * (N - 1) / 2$$

In most big companies, you'll find dozens of people assigned to a single project — creating hundreds of communication links. That complexity is the enemy of speed and creativity.

Your Rule of Thumb

If the team can't be fed with two pizzas, it's too big to innovate.

Keep it small, strong, and autonomous.

4. IMPLEMENT THE MOONSHOT THINKING

4.1. What is a Moonshot?

As you may be aware, a Moonshot is a mindset that encourages individuals to believe in achieving things that might seem impossible at first.

The term "moonshot thinking" was born in a speech by John F. Kennedy, where he dared the nation to achieve what seemed impossible: landing on the moon in under 10 years. Spoken in 1962, it became a reality when Neil Armstrong took that historic step a few years later.

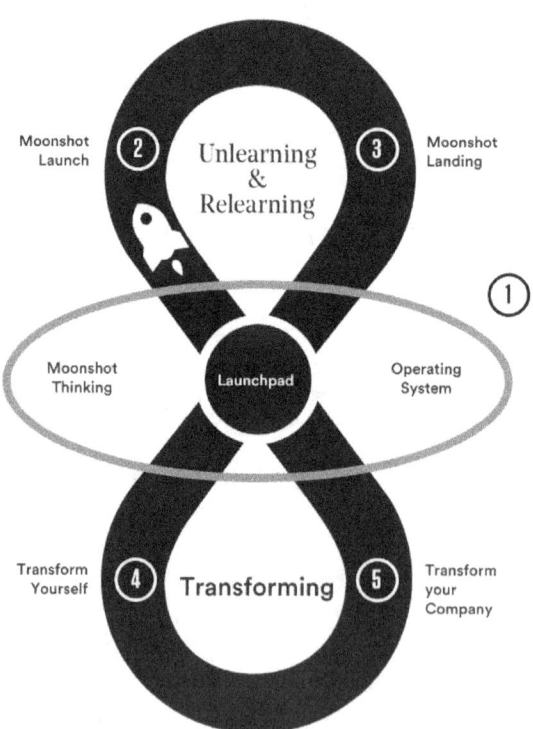

4.2. Advantages

Empowers unconventional solutions

Encourages fast-paced experimentation

Challenges established norms

Removes fear of failure, focusing on success

4.3. Beyond Theory

Waymo by Google: The Autonomous Odyssey - Google leaped with a dream - a car that could drive itself. Enter Waymo, the fully autonomous driving vehicle. Waymo can gracefully navigate a few miles sans a driver, showcasing the power of moonshot thinking on our roads.

Impossible Foods: Redefining Plant-Based Feasts - Imagine creating meat, fish, and dairy products from plants! Impossible Foods envisioned a world where delectable treats are crafted sustainably, without any harm to animals. Their moonshot goal? Replicating the taste of meat in a planet-friendly way.

Archinaut: Crafting Cosmic Structures - In the vastness of space, Archinaut aims high. Their mission? To build and assemble large-scale structures right there in the cosmos. Archinaut's journey embodies the spirit of moonshot thinking, reaching for the stars and constructing wonders beyond our planet.

These companies are living proof that moonshot thinking can turn audacious goals into tangible, groundbreaking realities.

4.4. How to Implement it

Embarking on a moonshot journey requires a strategic approach. Here's a practical 5-step framework to infuse Moonshot Thinking into your company:

- **Unleash Creativity**

    Build a space where teams can be really creative without limits. Make a culture that likes when people speak up, so everyone in the team can share their ideas, thoughts, and worries freely. Welcome different ways of thinking to come up with lots of ideas, and find amazing projects.

- **Assemble a Multi-Disciplinary Team**

    Put together teams with different skills and knowledge. When people with various backgrounds work together, they can look at goals from different angles and come up with creative ways to solve problems. Give your teams the tools and technology they need to turn their big ideas into reality.

- **Establish Essential Limits**

    When thinking about big and ambitious ideas, also recognize the risks involved. Set clear boundaries, like the most money you're willing to spend and the level of commitment the company is ready for. This makes sure that you're innovating responsibly within certain limits.

- **Set Challenging Objectives**

    Welcome big and challenging goals. Understand that you might make mistakes, but concentrate on what you learn and how you grow along the way. Every setback teaches you something important, adding to the overall success of the project.

- **Foster a Culture of Innovation**

    Create a place where your team can feel free to come up with bold and unusual ideas without worrying about making mistakes. Promote a culture that values trying new things, learns from problems, and sees challenges as chances to find amazing solutions. Make sure your team is open with each other, setting the stage for always coming up with new and innovative things.

4.5. Benefits

- **Personal and Professional Growth:**
    Participation in moonshot projects fosters fearlessness and empowerment, facilitating personal and professional growth.

- **Creativity and Motivation:**
  A team confident in their knowledge and skills generates an atmosphere of confidence and strength. This confidence breeds a desire to achieve the seemingly impossible, with each setback serving as a lesson in the journey.

5. DEFINE SUCCESS METRICS USING OKRS

If you can't measure it, you can't improve it. Every action plan should be tied to concrete, outcome-driven success metrics.

High alignment and high autonomy are the secrets of success. Let your team define how they will achieve success.

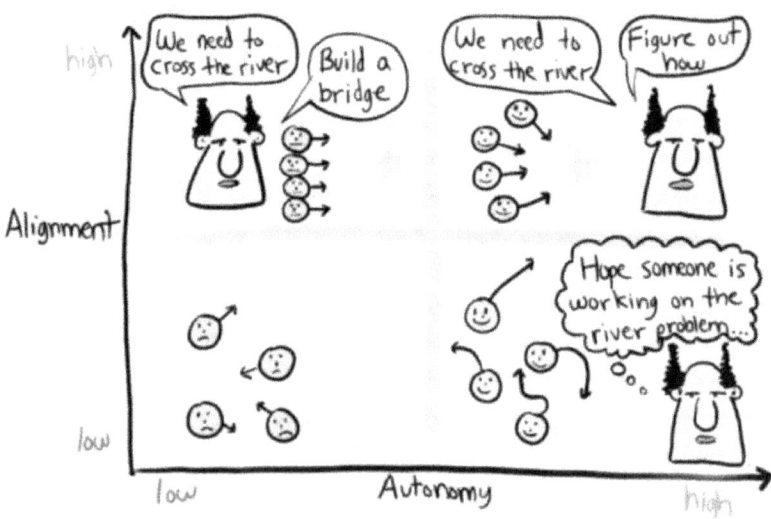

Use OKRs and embrace the Moonshot concept to drive your team beyond conventional boundaries.

Allow them to fail. Sooner or later, they will come up with a solution that provides a positive ROI. Heroes always find a way. And that's why we need them.

Objective: What is the ambitious goal we want to achieve?

Key Results: How will we measure progress in a quantifiable way?

For example:

Objective: Improve customer engagement in digital channels.

Key Results: Increase mobile app adoption by 30%, reduce churn by 20%, and improve CSAT scores to 90%.

OKRs help bridge the gap between strategy and execution, ensuring that innovation is not just happening in a bubble but is actively contributing to business impact.

At the end of this chapter, you will find a framework to help you define success metrics with OKRs.

6. SHIFT YOUR ORGANIZATION'S MINDSET

At the heart of innovation lies a fundamental mindset shift — from a fear of failure to an embrace of learning. This shift is critical for fostering an environment where rapid prototyping, iteration, and adaptation are part of the DNA.

6.1. From Project to Product

One of the biggest mindset shifts for traditional companies is transitioning from projects to products.

Project thinking: A fixed timeline, a defined scope, and a rigid launch plan.

Product thinking: A continuous, iterative cycle of improvement, learning, and adaptation.

Instead of spending years perfecting an idea in isolation, high-growth companies operate in perpetual beta, shipping Minimum Viable Products (MVPs) and refining them based on user feedback.

- **Key principles of a Product Mindset:**

    Ship small, learn fast - Adopt Baby Steps — gradual, incremental improvements rather than a high-risk Big Bang launch.

    Prioritize impact, not perfection - Focus on solving real pain points, not over-engineering features.

6.2. From Building to Last to Building to Change

For decades, traditional corporate strategy has been centered around the idea of "building to last"—creating rigid structures, long-term plans, and stable operational models designed for efficiency and predictability. While this approach was effective in stable markets, today's rapidly changing world demands a different way of thinking.

Companies that thrive today are not built to last in the conventional sense. They are built to evolve, to adapt, and to change continuously. The focus is no longer on longevity through rigid structures but on sustained relevance through agility.

- **Building to Last:** Companies create static business models, processes, and technologies designed for long-term stability.

- **Building to Change:** Companies design for adaptability, ensuring that their teams, products, and business models are flexible and ready to pivot.

Why Building to Change Matters

- Speed beats certainty – The best decision today is often better than the perfect decision next year.
- Customer expectations evolve quickly – If your systems, processes, and teams cannot adapt, your customers will leave for a more agile competitor.
- Technology moves fast – What worked five years ago is already obsolete. Companies must be ready to reinvent themselves.

How to Build for Change

- **Adopt modular systems** – Instead of monolithic platforms, build tech stacks that can be easily updated and integrated with new technologies.
- **Foster a culture of experimentation** – Encourage teams to test new ideas rapidly without fear of failure.
- **Embrace short feedback loops** – Implement agile methodologies that allow teams to adjust based on real-time customer feedback.

- **Invest in adaptable talent** – Hire and develop people who thrive in uncertain environments and are eager to learn new skills.

Example:

Building to Last: A telecom company invests in a decade-long infrastructure project with no flexibility to adjust to new customer demands.

Building to Change: The same telecom company launches a 5-year roadmap with iterative updates, allowing for pivots based on market needs and emerging technologies.

The companies that survive disruption are the ones designed for continuous reinvention.

6.3. From Big Bang to Baby Steps

My little daughter started walking. It's incredible how a human being evolves in just one year, going from 100% dependent to walking and talking on her own. People usually say: *"Enjoy it, because it goes by fast"*

The coolest part is that she learned to crawl, but now she doesn't do it. She picked up new skills during this phase and built something important for her growth, but she doesn't need it anymore.

This got me thinking about how big corporations drive organizational change. In the context of a big corporation, one year is considered a short-term horizon. Imagine if we approached organizational change like a baby taking baby steps. After just one year, you could see an amazing transformation. Can you picture it?

So stop focusing on Big Bang projects and start evolving like a baby.

Let's break it down:

- **Big Bang Projects**

    The Big Mess: Trying to change everything at once can get super messy. It's like throwing a massive party without planning – chaos alert!

    Taking Forever: Big projects often take ages to finish. The longer it takes, the more problems can pop up, and we all know time is money.

    Not Everyone's a Fan: Suddenly changing everything might freak people out. Employees might not be on board, making the whole thing a bit of a struggle.

- **Baby Steps**

    Incremental Progress: Taking small, incremental steps allows for steady progress, like crafting with building blocks. You start with a few, see how they fit together, and then add more as you go.

Adaptability: Small changes are often more adaptable to evolving circumstances, ensuring flexibility in the face of unforeseen challenges.

Employee Buy-In: Implementing changes gradually can foster better employee buy-in, as it provides time for everyone to adjust and embrace the shifts.

7. DON'T OVERENGINEER – SOLVE SMART, NOT HARD

7.1. Lean Startup

When I first came across the Lean Startup methodology, I realized it wasn't about running like a startup. It was about thinking like one — even inside a billion-dollar company.

The core principle? Don't guess. Test.

This doesn't mean launching junk. It means focusing on the riskiest assumptions first and testing them with real users before scaling.

Here's how I apply Lean Startup inside big companies:
- Start with a hypothesis, not a plan: "We believe X will improve Y because Z." Then go prove or disprove it.

- Build the smallest thing possible to test that hypothesis — sometimes it's a clickable prototype, a landing page, or even a concierge experiment.

- Measure what matters: Forget vanity metrics. Focus on behavioral data — did people sign up? Did they come back? Did they refer someone?

- Learn fast, pivot if needed, and only then scale.

Real-World Application:

I have used Lean Startup to test a digital service for patients. Instead of building an app upfront, we tested the idea using WhatsApp and a manual concierge team. Within two weeks, we had enough data to validate demand, improve the experience, and justify building a proper product. That saved us six months of guesswork.

I applied a similar Lean Startup approach during my time at Nextel. We wanted to validate customer interest in a new mobile plan, but instead of spending millions on traditional focus groups and market research — which often deliver slow, biased, or inconclusive results — we took a smarter route.

We launched a series of landing pages with a fake new telecom brand, each showcasing a different pricing structure and value proposition. Then, with just a few hundred dollars in targeted social media ads, we directed our ideal customers to those pages.

Within a few days, the data spoke louder than any boardroom debate. The conversion rates clearly revealed which offer resonated most with our audience—and more importantly, which ones didn't.

This quick, low-cost experiment gave us the clarity and confidence to move forward with the winning value proposition, avoiding wasted resources and accelerating our go-to-market decision.

That's the power of Lean: fast, customer-driven validation— without the drama.

7.2. Minimum Viable Products

You may have heard about MVPs, but let me dive deeper into corporate MVP challenges and dilemmas.

- **The Executive Dilemma: Fear of Imperfection**

    Let's tackle the myth that has long haunted big corporate executives — the fear of launching an MVP that might destroy their reputation and the company's polished brand image.

    In the corporate world, executives often shy away from the notion of unveiling an MVP, fearing that a less-than-perfect product might risk their career and the company's brand reputation. It's the classic battle between the pursuit of excellence and the willingness to embrace imperfection.

Let's explore real stories of big corporations that defied the odds and embraced MVPs, paving the way for innovation and market disruption.

- **Amazon's Kindle Journey**

When Amazon introduced the Kindle, it wasn't the sophisticated e-reader we know today. However, it disrupted the traditional publishing industry and laid the foundation for future advancements. Imperfection led to innovation.

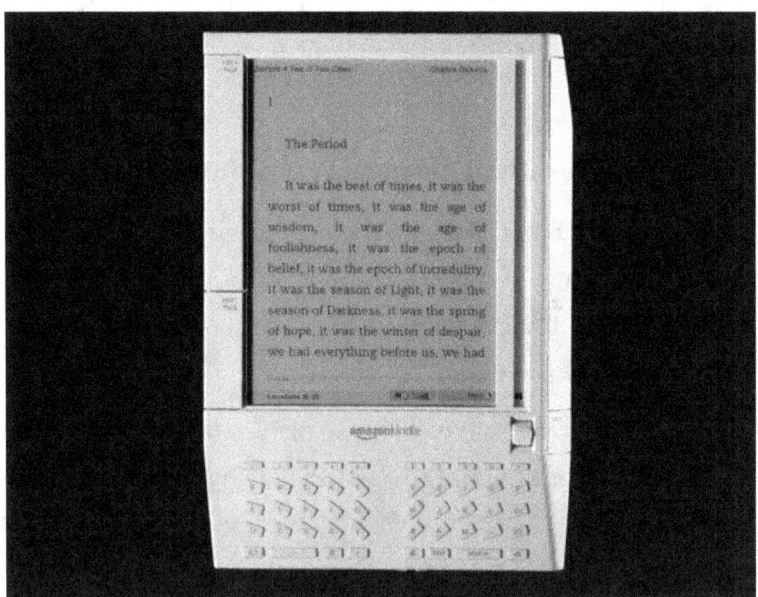

The inaugural Kindle: a device with chunky angles, buttons reminiscent of slabs, and an aggressively ergonomic keyboard

- **Apple's iPhone Photo App**

    Even a tech giant like Apple, known for its sleek and polished products, had humble beginnings with its first iPhone. While Nokia and Blackberry had video, zoom, and advanced features, the first iPhone photo app had only one button: take a picture. That simple. Nothing else. But the impact it made was revolutionary.

    Sometimes, imperfection is the birthplace of innovation.

    Embrace imperfection. If they did, you can do it too!

Benefits of MVPs

The cost of MVP development has significantly dropped with low-code and no-code drag-and-drop solutions.

Developing a first version of your solution is so affordable that it's worth the risk of testing it with real users instead of going through extensive research, prototyping, building, and launching.

Just build and launch!

- Risk Mitigation: MVPs allow organizations to test ideas with minimal risk before committing extensive resources.

- Speed to Market: By adopting an agile approach, big corps can accelerate the time it takes to bring innovative solutions to the market.

- Cost-Efficiency: Focusing on the core features in an MVP minimizes unnecessary costs and resources, optimizing the innovation process.

- Customer-Centric Innovation: Gathering feedback early and often ensures that products align closely with customer needs and preferences.

7.2. Design Thinking, Sprints & Jams

Design Thinking: A mindset shift from product-first to people-first

At its core, Design Thinking is about empathy — deeply understanding your user's pain points before jumping to solutions. Instead of assuming what people need, you co-create with them.

In practice, Design Thinking helps you:

- Explore the problem space before defining the solution
- Involve real users early and often
- Rapidly prototype and test ideas with minimal waste

I used this approach at a healthcare company to improve patient adherence to treatment. Instead of hiring another consultancy, we sat with real patients, mapped their frustrations, and co-created simple tools to reduce drop-offs. The solution wasn't a new app — it was a new reminder protocol and simplified instructions.

- **Design Sprints: Solve a big challenge in just 5 days**

    Originally developed by Google Ventures, Design Sprints are a structured, time-boxed process to go from idea to tested prototype in just one week.

    When I want to cut through corporate noise and get results fast, this is my go-to format.

    In a typical sprint, you:
    - Map the challenge
    - Sketch solutions
    - Decide the best one
    - Build a realistic prototype
    - Test with real users

    At Dasa, we used a sprint to test a concept for a unified health dashboard. Instead of spending months building a roadmap, we aligned key stakeholders in one room, prototyped a solution in 48 hours, and tested it with doctors by day five. That test gave us clarity to move forward or pivot — before writing a single line of code.

- **Design Jams: Creative problem-solving at startup speed**

If Design Thinking is a mindset and Design Sprints are a structured process, Design Jams are your creative sandbox. They're intense, collaborative workshops designed to generate ideas and validate them quickly — often in a single day.

I use Design Jams when:

- I need fresh thinking on a known problem
- The team is stuck in analysis paralysis
- There's little budget, but urgency is high

One of the most impactful outcomes I've seen from a single Design Jam happened when my team reimagined something as "boring" as a digital invoice.

We gathered designers, developers, and customer service reps in one room and ran a full-day Jam focused on a single question: Why are so many people calling the call center after receiving their invoice?

By the end of the session, we had prototyped a simplified invoice design — clearer layout, better explanations, and proactive answers to common questions. We tested it with real users, refined it quickly, and rolled it out.

The result? A 15% drop in call center inquiries, translating into millions in annual savings. All from one Design Jam. No big budgets. No endless meetings. Just focused collaboration, fast learning, and execution.

Here are three different approaches combined to enhance your gradual progress on new projects and initiatives for your company: Design Thinking + Lean Startup + Agile.

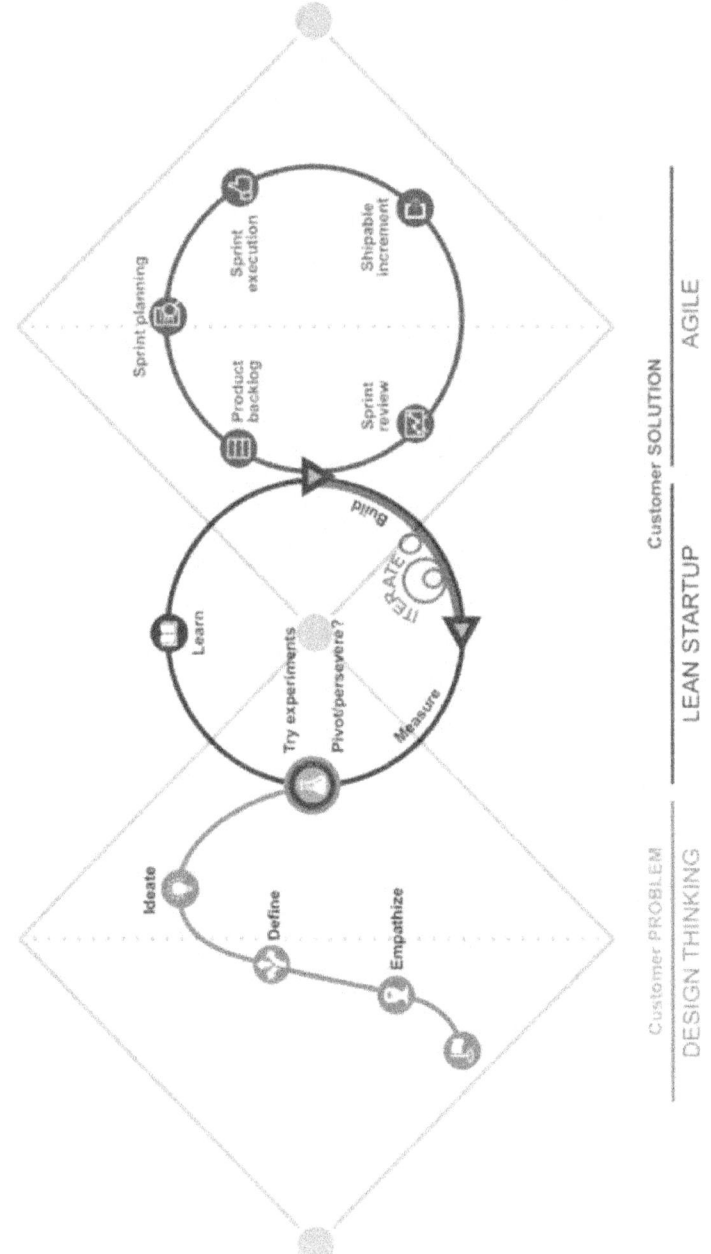

8. MEASURE CUSTOMER SATISFACTION

Measuring customer satisfaction is critical to ensuring that your innovations are well-received and impactful. It allows you to gauge the effectiveness of your initiatives and make data-driven decisions to enhance customer experiences continuously.

Here is an easy way for you to use NPS (Net Promote Score) to simplify the process.

NPS is based on one primary question: "On a scale of 0 to 10, how likely are you to recommend our product/service to a friend or colleague?" Customers' responses classify them into three categories:

- Promoters (9-10): Loyal enthusiasts who will keep buying and refer others.
- Passives (7-8): Satisfied but unenthusiastic customers who are vulnerable to competitive offerings.
- Detractors (0-6): Unhappy customers who can damage your brand and impede growth through negative word-of-mouth.

The NPS is calculated by subtracting the percentage of Detractors from the percentage of Promoters:

NPS = % Promoters − % Detractors

8.1. Implementing NPS: A Step-by-Step Guide

- **Survey Design:**

  Include the primary NPS question.

  Add open-ended follow-up questions to gather qualitative feedback.

- **Data Collection:**

  Use various channels like email, SMS, or in-app surveys to reach customers.

  Ensure the timing of the survey is appropriate (e.g., after a purchase or service interaction).

- **Analysis:**

  Categorize responses into Promoters, Passives, and Detractors.

  Calculate the NPS score.

  Analyze qualitative feedback to identify common themes and areas for improvement.

- **Action Plan:**

  Promoters: Engage and reward loyal customers. Encourage them to become brand advocates.

  Passives: Identify ways to convert them into Promoters by enhancing their experience.

  Detractors: Address their concerns promptly and work to resolve issues to improve their experience.

- **Continuous Improvement:**

    Regularly measure NPS to track progress over time.

    Use the feedback to drive continuous improvement in products, services, and customer interactions.

8.2. Survey Template:

NPS Question:

"On a scale of 0 to 10, how likely are you to recommend our product/service to a friend or colleague?"

Follow-Up Questions:

"What is the primary reason for your score?"

"What can we do to improve your experience?"

8.3. Actionable Steps for Improvement

- Engage Promoters:
- Implement a referral program.
- Create exclusive offers or loyalty rewards.

- **Convert Passives:**

    Enhance customer support and service.

Personalize their experience based on feedback.

- **Address Detractors:**

    Contact detractors to understand and resolve their issues.

    Implement changes based on their feedback to prevent recurrence.

9. ALIGN DIGITAL, IT & BUSINESS

Every digital transformation I've led has had one common friction point: the blurry boundaries between digital, marketing, and IT.

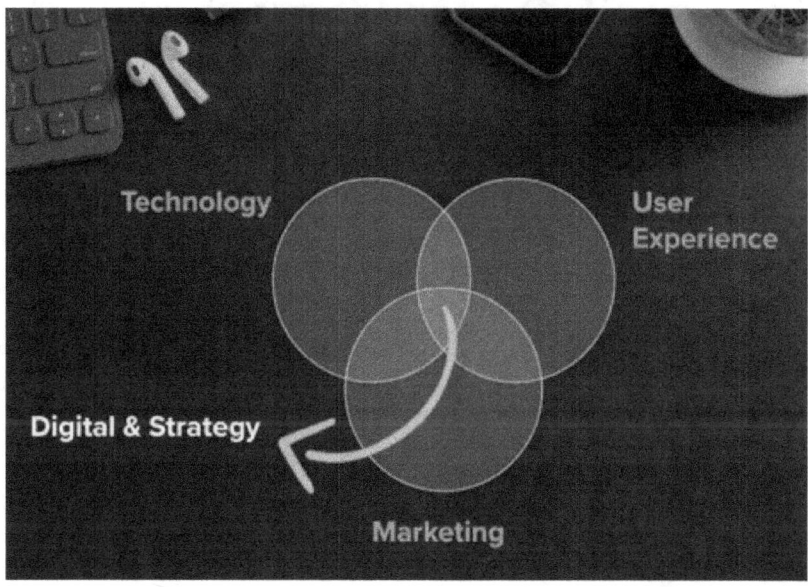

This disconnect often leads to power struggles between Chief Digital Officers (CDOs) and CTOs, delaying execution. To break this deadlock, we need a new approach to IT in innovation.

9.1. Evolve IT from Support to Strategic

Many traditional IT teams operate in support mode, focusing on keeping systems stable. However, in a digital-first world, IT must evolve into a strategic enabler.

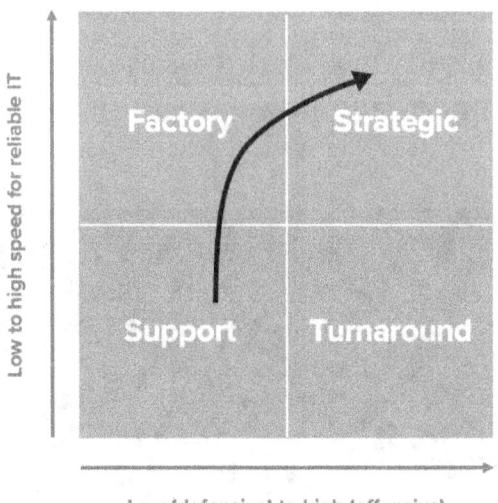

Support Mode: Standardized platforms, stable operations.

Strategic Mode: Rapid iterations, in-house development capabilities.

To avoid conflicts, separate your systems into distinct layers. Each layer has a specific mission, team, and governance.

I like using this framework to guide the change:

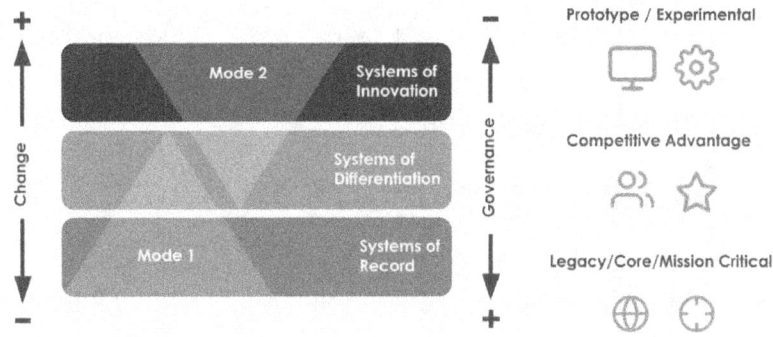

Usually, as a digital leader, you have to work hard to set up Systems of Innovation Layers and teams. They won't be there when you start your Digital Transformation journey.

To ensure success, you need to establish a Prototype/Experimental layer led by the digital innovation team, closely aligned with the IT team.

The digital innovation team should concentrate on testing novel approaches to attract, convert, and retain new customers, while the IT team should focus on Legacy, Core, and Mission-Critical systems.

During these tests, it's not uncommon to encounter disruptions in other layers' systems. This underscores the importance of aligning expectations (and being explicit about the potential influx of unexpected new visitors in the systems).

Pro Tip - These teams have very different goals. Sometimes, they have opposite and conflicting reasons and ways of thinking. So, it's crucial to keep them separate and define different metrics and KPIs to track their performance.

Digital: front-end customer experience innovation. This team needs freedom to create.

IT: back-end critical systems operation. This team needs system stability.

Here is a table to guide you in creating/adapting and leading these teams:

SYSTEMS OF RECORDS	SYSTEMS OF INNOVATION
Core IT	Digital Innovation
Build to last	Build to change
Standardization	Customization
Processes and efficiency	Experimentation and cash burn
Hire people to execute the plan	Hire people to figure out the plan
Command & control	Freedom & responsibility
SMART goals	Moonshot goals
Common ideas	New ideas
Current mission-critical	Next competitive advantage
Compliance	Respect the law, challenge rules

The idea here is to equip you with executive knowledge so you can understand, negotiate, build, and make these different systems coexist harmoniously.

10. DRIVE GROWTH IMPLEMENTING A FUNNEL STRATEGY

Pirate Metrics, or AARRR (Acquisition, Activation, Retention, Referral, and Revenue), provide a clear framework for understanding customer behavior and optimizing their journey for growth.

Here's how I customize this approach for a large-scale operation:

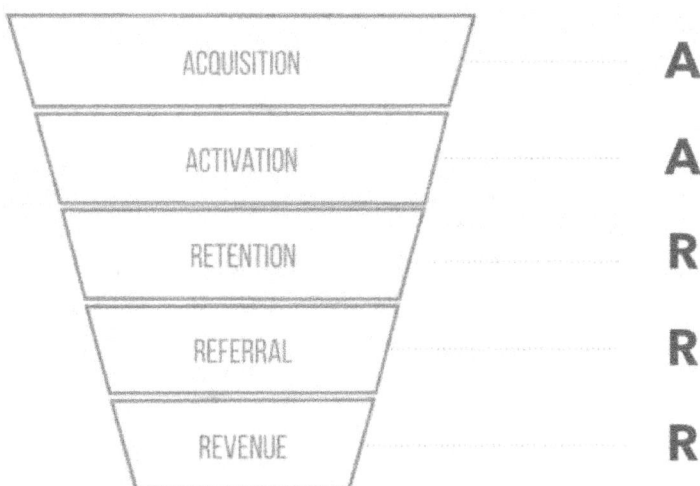

Acquisition:

I target not just more customers, but the right customers. By leveraging big data and predictive analytics, I identify and pursue segments that offer the highest growth potential.

Funnel Metrics:

3. Customer acquisition cost (per channel)
4. Conversion rate
5. Traffic driven to the website (per channel)
6. Click-through rate
7. Cost per click
8. Dwell time on website
9. Bounce rates
10. Quality of leads

Activation:

Making a great first impression is crucial. I refine onboarding processes to ensure that the first interaction with the product is both intuitive and fulfilling.

Funnel Metrics:

11. Time to value
12. Visitors to registration ratio
13. Conversion rate
14. How many customers used a crucial product feature?

15. How many customers experienced the AHA moment?
16. Drop-off rate
17. Dwell time + viewed pages

Retention:

This is where most big corporations fail. I implement continuous engagement tactics, using personalized communications and AI-driven insights to keep offerings relevant.

Funnel Metrics:

18. Retention rate vs. churn rate
19. Open rate of emails
20. Click trough rate of emails
21. Customer churn
22. Month to recover CAC
23. Average customer retention length (time people stay active customers)
24. Net Promoter Score
25. Infrequent logins

Referral:

Encouraging satisfied customers to become brand advocates is a powerful growth lever. I use satisfaction scores to identify potential advocates and incentivize referrals, effectively turning the customer base into a growth engine.

Funnel Metrics:

26. Percentage of customers who refer friends
27. Referred customers
28. Percentage of total purchases by referred customers
29. Lifetime value of referred customers
30. Positive reviews
31. Social media shares
32. Sent invitations & successful invitations
33. Viral coefficient & viral cycle time
34. Net Promoter Score

Revenue:

By understanding the nuances of each customer's journey, I can tailor offerings and upsell effectively, increasing the customer lifetime value significantly.

Funnel Metrics:

35. Customer lifetime value
36. Customer acquisition cost
37. Monthly recurring revenue
38. How many free customers become paying customers?

39. Average order value per customer
40. Repeated purchases
41. Revenue churn
42. Expansion revenue

WORKING SESSION

Time to Set Up Your OKRs

In this session, you'll learn how to cascade your innovation vision into measurable, actionable goals. We'll break it down into three layers of OKRs — Company, Team, and Personal — so that everyone is aligned, from the C-suite to the frontline.

Why This Matters

By using this three-tier OKR model, you ensure:

Strategic alignment across all levels

Transparency of progress and priorities

A culture of accountability and outcome-driven thinking

Whether you're scaling a pilot or executing a moonshot, OKRs keep everyone focused on what matters most.

1. Company OKRs – Aligning Around Strategic Outcomes

At the top level, company OKRs reflect your strategic priorities — the core outcomes that will move the business forward. These objectives should be bold but focused, and they must directly support your reason to innovate and digital ambition (defined in Chapters 1 and 3).

Each Company Objective should have:

A clear, inspiring statement of what you want to achieve

3 measurable Key Results that show progress toward the objective

A regularly tracked progress score to measure fulfillment

Tip: Company OKRs guide everyone — they're not task lists, they're outcome statements. Avoid including operational to-do items.

Company OKRs Progress Tracker

		Objective fulfillment
Company Objective One	Progress	23%
Measurable key result 1	10%	
Measurable key result 2	20%	
Measurable key result 3	40%	

		Objective fulfillment
Company Objective Two	Progress	15%
Measurable key result 1	5%	
Measurable key result 2	15%	
Measurable key result 3	25%	

		Objective fulfillment
Company Objective Three	Progress	0%
Measurable key result 1	0%	
Measurable key result 2	0%	
Measurable key result 3	0%	

Total fulfillment across objectives	13%

2. Team OKRs – Driving Execution Within Squads

Team OKRs take the company objectives and break them into specific, actionable goals for each squad or department. These OKRs are about execution, tied to the flagship initiatives and pilots you selected earlier in the chapter.

Each squad should define:

An objective that connects to at least one Company Objective

3 Key Results tied to delivery metrics or customer outcomes

A progress tracker to promote accountability and visibility

Tip: In agile squads, allow teams autonomy to propose how they'll contribute. This increases ownership and motivation.

Team OKRs Progress Tracker

		Objective fulfillment
Team Objective One	Progress	23%
Measurable key result 1	10%	
Measurable key result 2	20%	
Measurable key result 3	40%	

		Objective fulfillment
Team Objective Two	Progress	15%
Measurable key result 1	5%	
Measurable key result 2	15%	
Measurable key result 3	25%	

		Objective fulfillment
Team Objective Three	Progress	0%
Measurable key result 1	0%	
Measurable key result 2	0%	
Measurable key result 3	0%	

Total fulfillment across objectives	13%

3. Personal OKRs – Empowering Individuals with Clarity and Purpose

Finally, Personal OKRs translate the team's goals into individual focus. These are especially useful for digital innovation squads, where roles are often fluid and impact-oriented.

Each person should define:

One or two personal objectives connected to their squad's OKRs

2-3 Key Results to guide their weekly efforts

A self-tracked progress metric to encourage self-leadership

Tip: Make OKRs part of 1:1s and performance conversations, not just annual reviews. Use them as coaching tools, not evaluation checklists.

Personal OKRs Progress Tracker

		Objective fulfillment
Personal Objective One	**Progress**	**23%**
Measurable key result 1	10%	
Measurable key result 2	20%	
Measurable key result 3	40%	

		Objective fulfillment
Personal Objective Two	**Progress**	**15%**
Measurable key result 1	5%	
Measurable key result 2	15%	
Measurable key result 3	25%	

		Objective fulfillment
Personal Objective Three	**Progress**	**0%**
Measurable key result 1	0%	
Measurable key result 2	0%	
Measurable key result 3	0%	

Total fulfillment across objectives	13%

6. OPTIMIZATION

TLDR

This chapter helps you optimize your innovation engine by managing it as a measurable portfolio. You'll explore digital business models and platform strategies, structure your initiatives into three horizons, and track performance using the Innovation Funnel. Finally, the Innovation Sonar helps map ownership, effort, and business impact — giving you clarity to prioritize what matters and scale what works.

PORTFOLIO MANAGEMENT AND CONTINUOUS INNOVATION PROCESS

Digital technology has revolutionized traditional business models, paving the way for innovative approaches that leverage connectivity, data, and automation. There are various business models enabled by digital advancements.

1. EXPLORE NEW BUSINESS MODELS

E-Commerce

E-commerce involves buying and selling goods via the internet. Key benefits include broad reach, availability, cost efficiency, enhanced customer experience, and segmentation. E-commerce platforms typically maintain proprietary inventory, offering convenience and wide product selection to consumers.

Market Place Match Making

This model facilitates transactions between buyers and sellers, creating a marketplace without holding inventory. Key advantages are cost savings, efficient payment processing, synergies, and strategic positioning. Platforms like Airbnb connect users directly, providing a decentralized approach to commerce.

SaaS (Software as a Service)

Companies license applications on demand, offering automatic updates, speed, customization, and integration. SaaS reduces the need for on-premise infrastructure, providing scalable and flexible solutions to businesses.

Subscription

This model involves selling access to products or services for a recurring fee. Benefits include a stable customer base, consumer consumption patterns, continuous development (beta features), and recurring revenue streams.

User Generated Content

Platforms relying on user-generated content allow users to produce and share their own content. This model benefits from extensive reach, segmentation, cost efficiency, and user feedback, primarily generating revenue through advertising.

Media Site

Media sites create or curate content, monetizing through advertising. These platforms focus on reach, segmentation, and user feedback to tailor content to specific audiences and attract advertisers.

Apps

Mobile applications provide direct communication channels, user interaction, and availability. Apps offer various monetization strategies, including service fees, subscriptions, and in-app purchases, enhancing user convenience and engagement.

2. GET TO KNOW PLATFORM STRATEGIES

Platform strategies are essential for businesses aiming to harness the power of network effects and create value by facilitating exchanges between different user groups. These strategies can transform traditional business models by leveraging digital technologies.

Large corporations often focus on substantial investments and grand projects, but there is much to learn from startups like LinkedIn, PayPal, and Uber. These companies began with small, manageable projects, delivering strong value while incrementally developing their platform strategies. By taking baby steps and focusing on core functionalities, they were able to grow sustainably and effectively.

Let's dive a bit into LinkedIn's launch and growth platform strategy:

Minimum Viable Platform (MVP)

A Minimum Viable Platform focuses on the core functionalities needed to address the primary needs of its users. The goal is to achieve the essence of what the platform aims to do, facilitating one interaction at a time.

Key Elements of an MVP:

- Core Functionality: Start with the basic features that address the main user needs.

- Iterative Development: Continuously improve based on user feedback and data.

- Scalability: Design to support future growth and additional features.

Transition from One-Sided to Multi-Sided Platforms

A one-sided platform serves a single user group, while a multi-sided platform connects two or more distinct but interdependent user groups, enhancing value through network effects.

Example: LinkedIn Case Study

- One-Sided Platform: Initially focused on professionals creating profiles.
- Multi-Sided Platform: Expanded to include recruiters, advertisers, and thought leaders.

Steps to Transition:

Profile Creation: Allow professionals to create detailed profiles.

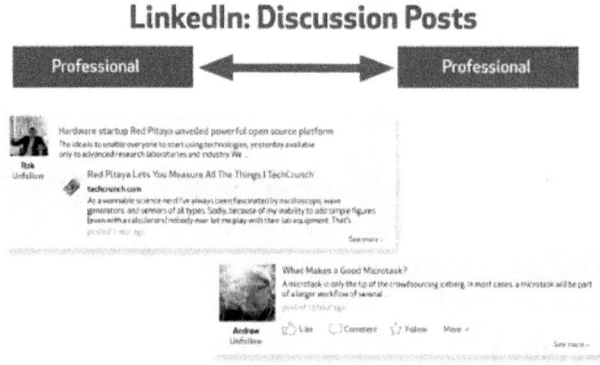

Discussion Posts: Enable interaction and knowledge sharing among professionals.

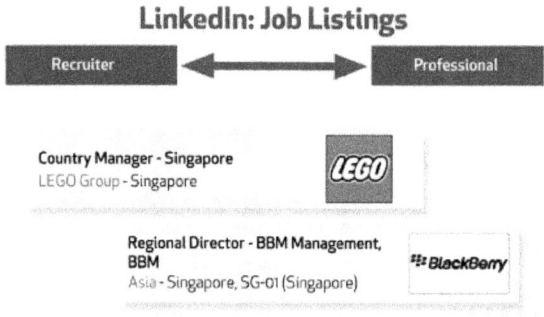

Job Listings: Connect professionals with recruiters through job postings.

Thought Leadership Insights: Provide a space for thought leaders to share insights, attracting advertisers seeking targeted audiences.

Benefits of Platform Strategies

- Network Effects: Each new user adds value to the platform for existing users.
- Scalability: Platforms can grow exponentially as more users join.
- Data Utilization: Platforms can leverage data to improve services and personalize user experiences.
- Revenue Streams: Multiple revenue streams through subscriptions, advertisements, and premium services.

3. STRUCTURE A PLANNING & GOVERNANCE PROCESS

3.1. Break Your Innovation Plan Into Three Horizons

Efficiently managing innovation initiatives to maximize results and achieve business goals.

The basic balance of a portfolio is 70 / 20 / 10. However, it depends a lot on whether the business is in an attack or defense position.

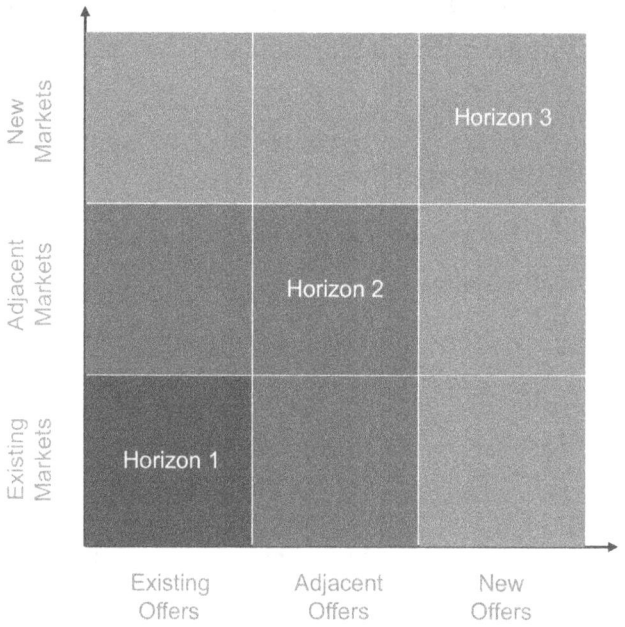

Companies in a defense position must focus efforts on horizons 1 and 2, as their survival is at risk.

On the other hand, companies with cash health, and which are not suffering short/medium-term threats or risks, can and should invest in the horizon 3

Horizon 1:

Time: Short Term

Scope: Core Business

Focus: Exploration and optimization of existing businesses

Metrics: ROI, NPV

Team: Maintainers

Capacity: Existing

Horizon 2:

Time: Medium Term

Scope: Growth Business

Focus: Expanding existing businesses and building adjacent innovations

Metrics: Innovation Accounting

Team: Intrapreneur, Builder

Capacity: To be developed or acquired

Horizon 3:

Time: Long Term

Scope: Future Business

Focus: Exploration of new businesses, small bets on emerging opportunities, radical innovation

Metrics: Innovation Accounting

Team: Explorer, Adventurer, Intrapreneur

Capacity: Uncertain requirements

3.2. Define Metrics & KPIs For Each Initiative

Finally, it is crucial to measure the performance of the innovation as a whole.

The main innovation management metrics can be divided into 3 groups:

Field Metrics

- Number of ideas generated
- Number of MVPs developed
- Validation Speed
- Number of Experiments

Governance Metrics

- Number of projects in the pipeline
- Number of projects per innovation horizon
- % of projects in each phase of the innovation pipeline

Global Metrics

- ROII (Return on Innovation Investment)
- $ Reduction in operating cost
- $ Profits from innovation

Here is a bank of metrics to help you on the journey of choosing what to measure and how:

Field Metrics

Numbers of generated ideas
Number of ideas chosen
Number of hypotheses
Number of MVP's developed
Number of hypotheses
number of experiments
Number of interactions with customers
Number of interviews
Risky hypotheses identified
Hypotheses developed
Experiment results
cost per learning
Validation Speed
Pirate Metrics

Governance Metrics

Number of projects in the pipeline
Number of projects by horizons
Number of projects by innovation stage
Average spend per stage gate
% of projects aligned with the investment thesis
% of projects in the problem-solution phase
% of projects in the product-market fit part
% of products in scale
Number of Business Model Validations

Global Metrics

New Product/Service Revenue
ROI
Number of employees involved
Number of mentors
$ Reduction in operating cost
$ Profits from innovation
Number of new markets
market share number
Customer Satisfaction - NPS

Source Book The Corporate Startup

3.3. Measure The Success Rate of Your Initiatives

The Innovation Funnel:

This tool helps you track how your innovation initiatives progress — from initial idea to full adoption — and provides a clear picture of your success rate.

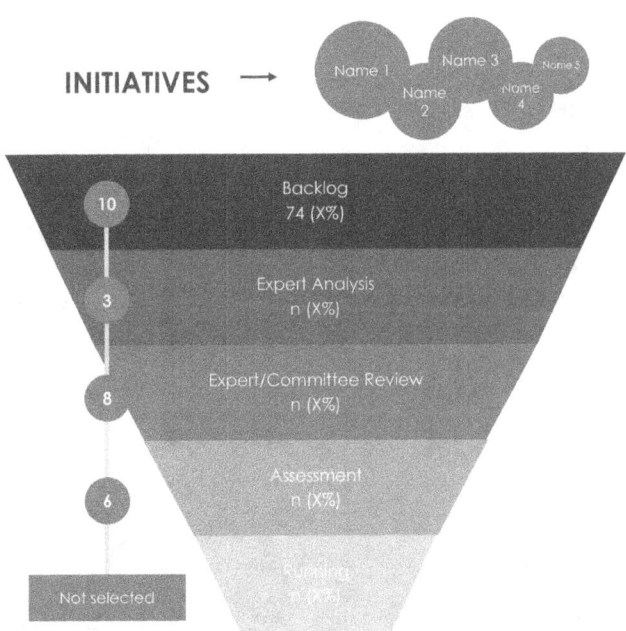

The Innovation Funnel is a visual tracker that plots all your innovation initiatives along two core metrics:

- Adoption Rate: How many initiatives are successfully implemented and embraced by the business?

- Mortality Rate: How many initiatives die along the way, whether due to lack of traction, technical challenges, or strategic misalignment?

A healthy innovation portfolio includes experiments that succeed and others that fail fast, generating insight and freeing up resources for better bets.

How to Use It:

- **List Your Initiatives:**

    Add each innovation initiative to the funnel, using real project names (or pseudonyms for discretion) to track their journey. Example: Digital Wallet, AI Support Bot, New Customer Onboarding Flow, etc.

- **Track Outcomes:**

    For each initiative, assign: An adoption status (e.g., fully adopted, partially adopted, on hold, or killed).

    A mortality reason, if the initiative was stopped — Was it due to lack of ROI? Technical debt? Low engagement?

- **Calculate Success Metrics:**

    Adoption Rate = (Number of Adopted Initiatives ÷ Total Initiatives) × 100

    Mortality Rate = (Number of Terminated Initiatives ÷ Total Initiatives) × 100

- **Review Periodically:**

    Run quarterly reviews with your Innovation Committee. Update progress, re-score initiatives if needed, and reflect on what's working and what's not.

Why This Works

This framework brings clarity to a space often filled with ambiguity. Instead of reporting just the number of MVPs launched or workshops held, you'll now be able to confidently answer:

How many initiatives became reality?

Where are we failing? Why?

What's the true ROI of our innovation effort?

It turns your innovation effort into a living portfolio — one that's measurable, actionable, and always evolving.

WORKING SESSION

Map Owners, Effort & Potential Impact

The Innovation Sonar:

This framework helps you visualize, prioritize, and align innovation initiatives based on four key dimensions:

- Who is Leading (Ownership)
- Implementation Cost (Effort)
- Business Impact (NPS - Net Present Value)
- Area of Focus (Balanced Outcomes)

It's an incredibly powerful tool for decision-making at scale, especially when your portfolio has multiple concurrent innovation initiatives.

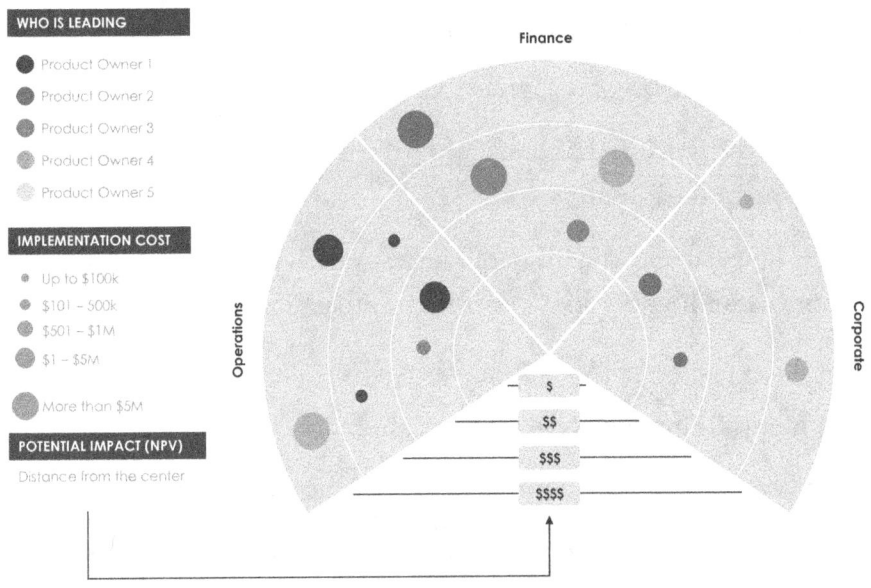

Framework Elements Explained:

1. Who Is Leading (Ownership)

Represented by colors or segments in the visual.

Indicates which area, department, or squad is responsible for the initiative.

Helps clarify accountability and ensure that every innovation effort has a clear owner.

How to use it: Assign colors to represent business different owners or teams. This helps quickly identify if some areas are overloaded or not contributing enough to innovation.

2. Implementation Cost (Effort)

Shown by the size of the circle (bubble).

The larger the bubble, the higher the estimated cost or effort to implement the initiative.

How to use it: Quickly filter out large initiatives that may not justify their cost or identify low-effort/high-impact ideas for quick wins.

3. Potential Impact (Net Present Value)

Represented by the distance from the center of the pie chart.

Measures the estimated Net Present Value (NPV) or business impact of the initiative.

How to use it: Focus on initiatives placed far from the center, as these are expected to deliver more significant value. Combine this with cost (size of each circle) to prioritize ROI.

4. Area of Focus (Balanced Outcomes)

Represented by the slices of the pie chart.

Maps which department or business area the innovation initiative is intended to impact.

How to use it: Quickly visualize which areas of the company are receiving the most innovation attention. Use this to identify if any departments are overloaded or underrepresented — and strategically rebalance your efforts and investments accordingly.

BONUS MATERIAL & WHAT'S NEXT

EXTRA RESOURCES FOR YOU TO SUCCEED

1. MY PERSPECTIVE ON THE GENERATIVE AI IMPACT

Whenever I need to understand what might happen in the future, I tend to look at lessons learned from past history. This is my humble approach.

By drawing a parallel between the industrial revolution and the technological revolution, you can see how technological advancements, whether in the past or present, initially increase workforce demand during the setup and expansion phases but eventually lead to a reduction in workforce needs as efficiency and automation take over. This perspective contextualizes the current technological changes within a broader historical framework.

1.1. Industrial Revolution

Initial Increase in Workforce Demand:

- **Setup and Expansion:** The early stages of the Industrial Revolution required a large workforce to build factories, infrastructure, and machinery. Many people moved from rural areas to urban centers to work in newly established industries.

- **Labor-Intensive Processes:** Early industrial processes were labor-intensive, relying heavily on human labor for production, transportation, and maintenance.

Technological Advancements:

- Mechanization and Automation: As technology advanced, machines began to take over many tasks previously done by hand. The introduction of steam engines, power looms, and other machinery increased productivity but started to reduce the need for manual labor.
- Skill Shifts: The nature of work changed, requiring new skills and leading to the rise of specialized labor. This created new job opportunities in machine operation, maintenance, and engineering.

Long-Term Workforce Reduction:

- Efficiency and Productivity: Increased efficiency and productivity meant fewer workers were needed to produce the same amount of goods. This led to job displacement in certain sectors.
- New Economic Opportunities: While some jobs were lost, new industries and sectors emerged, creating different types of employment opportunities.

1.2. Technological Revolution

Initial Increase in Workforce Demand:

- Setup and Expansion: Similar to the Industrial Revolution, the Technological Revolution has seen an initial increase in workforce demand to develop, implement, and maintain new technologies such as information technology infrastructure, artificial intelligence, robotics, and digital platforms.

- Tech-Driven Jobs: The rise of tech-driven industries has created a demand for jobs in software development, cybersecurity, data analysis, and other tech-related fields.

Technological Advancements:

- Automation and AI: Advances in artificial intelligence, machine learning, and robotics are automating many tasks that were previously done by humans. This includes not only manual labor but also routine cognitive tasks.
- Skill Shifts: The workforce is shifting towards more technical and specialized roles. There is a growing demand for skills in technology, critical thinking, and complex problem-solving.

Long-Term Workforce Reduction:

- Efficiency and Productivity: Similar to the Industrial Revolution, increased efficiency and productivity from automation and AI can lead to a reduction in the need for human labor in certain sectors.
- New Economic Opportunities: While some jobs are displaced, new industries and roles are emerging in areas

such as renewable energy, biotechnology, and advanced manufacturing.

1.3. Bridging the Two Revolutions

- Workforce Transition: Both revolutions require a transition period where the workforce must adapt to new technologies and job requirements. This often involves reskilling and upskilling.
- Economic Shifts: In both cases, the economy shifts from being labor-intensive to technology-intensive, changing the landscape of job opportunities and economic structures.
- Societal Impact: Both revolutions bring significant societal changes, including urbanization, changes in work-life balance, and shifts in social structures.

As we reflect on transformative innovations from the steam engine to artificial intelligence, the distinct feature of today's technological revolution is the breathtaking speed and the convergence of advancements. This era is not just another wave. It's an all-encompassing tsunami of change, arriving with unparalleled velocity.

1.4. Key Takeaways from AI Predictions

After reading the AI predictions from several top institutions, here are my takeaways:

- **Unprecedented Growth in Tech:** The world of AI is growing fast, with lots of money being invested and companies like NVIDIA becoming worth over $1 trillion. This shows how important AI is becoming in different types of work.

- **Societal Transformation:** Generative AI and big computer programs are expected to change our daily lives a lot, similar to how smartphones did. But there are challenges too, like people losing jobs, the problem of fake videos (deepfakes), and the gap between those who have access to digital resources and those who don't.

- **Revolutionizing Business Operations:** Gen AI is going to make it easier for everyone to use data, help people get more work done, and come up with new ways for businesses to talk to customers and deliver services. This means companies need to have good plans for using data safely and effectively.

- **Redefinition of Technical Roles:** AI is going to change the kind of work tech people do, making some tasks automatic but also creating chances for people to do more creative and important work, which might make people happier and more efficient at their jobs.

- **Cybersecurity Challenges and Opportunities:** With Gen AI, there are new problems and opportunities in keeping information safe. We'll need good AI tools for security, and we have to manage data well.

- **Widespread Technological Innovation:** Besides Gen AI, there are exciting developments in self-driving cars, better batteries, and biology technology that could change our world in big ways.

- **Economic Impact:** AI tools that people use directly could bring in a lot of money, possibly adding between $2.6 and $4.4 trillion to the world's economy every year. This means it's important for businesses to make smart choices about how they use and manage AI.

- **AI Adoption Across Industries:** Gen AI is so flexible that it's starting to be used in all parts of work, from talking to customers automatically to setting prices and helping with creative projects.

- **Data Infrastructure and Model Strategies:** To use AI well, we need a strong setup for storing and managing data, with something called data lakehouses being a good option because they are flexible and can grow. Deciding whether to make your own AI programs or use ones made by others, and choosing between open-source and owned technologies, are big decisions.

- **Governance and Ethical Considerations:** Running AI in a good and fair way means dealing with privacy, owning ideas, making sure data is reliable, and being able to explain how AI decisions are made. Doing AI the right way and having strong rules are important for avoiding problems.

- **Competitive Necessity and Strategic Foresight:** For businesses to stay in the game, they need to use Gen AI smartly. They have to be good at seeing what risks and chances AI brings and make wise plans for using it responsibly.

2. DEMYSTIFYING AI FOR NOT-TECH LEADERS

2.1. Main types and a brief explanation:

- **Artificial intelligence (AI):** A broad field that includes anything related to making machines smart.
- **Machine learning (ML):** A subset of AI that involves systems that can learn by themselves by identifying patterns.
- **Deep learning (DL):** A subset of ML that uses models built on deep neural networks to detect patterns with minimal human involvement.
- **Natural language processing (NLP):** The branch of AI focused on teaching machines to understand, interpret, and generate human language.

2.2. The AI journey and where we are now:

1942: Enigma broken with AI

1950: Test for machine intelligence by Alan Turing

1955: The father of AI - John McArthy

1964: The first chatbot - Eliza

1995: The chatbot ALICE

1997: DeepBlue beats chess legend

1998: The emotionally equipped robot - Kismet

2008: Voice recognition feature

2011: The Q/A computer system - IBM Watson

2020: Automated conversations - GPT models

Nowadays: AI combination & integration boom! It's used in autonomous vehicles, healthcare, finance, recommendation systems, generating new images, movie dubbing... We're on the cusp of AI breakthroughs in quantum computing, robotics, and more.

3. HOW TO MASTER GEN AI IMPLEMENTATION

The implementation of Artificial Intelligence (AI) and Machine Learning (ML) marks a pivotal era of transformation. Much like the cloud revolution, AI and ML are reshaping the landscape, uncovering insights hidden within our data.

With most tech decision-makers either embarking on or expanding their AI initiatives, the message is clear: the path to uncovering untapped insights begins with effective implementation. Here's the framework I've embraced to navigate this journey:

- **Identify Potential AI Use Cases:** Start with the magic question, "What problem are we trying to solve?" This problem statement will guide your exploration.

- **Set Objectives and KPIs:** Define your value hypothesis and quantify the expected business impact.

- **Prioritize:** Score your use-case ideas based on their business value and feasibility to ensure focus and alignment.

- **Data Quality and Availability:** Confirm that you have access to the necessary data, prioritizing quality over quantity.

- **Pilot Decision Point:** Evaluate whether to proceed with the pilot based on its potential impact and the data available.

- **Build and Validate Your Model:** Focus on testing your hypothesis, incorporating insights from a diverse group of experts.

- **Scale Decision Point:** Based on the validation phase, decide whether to scale the solution or explore another pilot.

- **Continuous Improvement:** Keep your model relevant by monitoring and updating it to adapt to market changes.

Generative AI is not just a trend; it's a transformative force that promises significant operational enhancements. Remember, this journey is a marathon, not a sprint. Start today and prepare to see the benefits unfold.

Next Steps: Build up a list of potential Generative AI experiments and discuss them with your leaders.

Use this table template sample to map, and track your progress.

What Problem We Are Trying to Solve?	Solution Statement / Business Goal	How Generative AI Can Transform	Sample Use Cases	Prioritization Score (0 to 10)		Data Access Score (0 to 10)	After Evaluating Feasibility, Impact and Data Accessibility, Should We Invest In The Pilot?	After Evaluating The Pilot Results, Should We Invest in Scaling It?
				Feasibility	Business Value			
Customers are not happy, low NPS	Improve Customer Satisfaction	Customers will expect personalized and immediate responses through generative AI interfaces, like a chat feature in our customer support channel.	- Use text generation to draft customer service responses - Chatbot - Sentiment analysis based on the customer interaction history	8	10	7	YES	YES
Our employees are not as productive as they could be	Increase employee productivity	Generative AI can accelerate technology creation improving developers productivity Employees can be supported with AI-powered assistants for many tasks (code, design, customer service interactions, check internal guidelines etc.)	- Code generation to improve developers productivity - Employee chatbot linked to knowledge repository - Search and summarize legal documents	8	9	6	YES	YES
We need to increase our revenue	Top-line revenue growth	Create personalized campaigns and content to attract and convert potential clients	- Create a buyer persona - Create persuasive text and images for personalized campaigns - Create product description drafts	7	8	9	YES	YES

4. WHAT'S NEXT

Congratulations on making it to the end of this journey. If you've reached this point, it means you've taken a bold step: not just to understand innovation, but to lead it.

Throughout this book, we've explored a proven 6-step method, practical frameworks, and real-life case studies to help you drive digital innovation in complex, traditional environments. You now have the tools, the mindset, and the roadmap. What comes next is where the real magic happens — putting it into practice, adapting it to your context, and evolving it as the world changes around us.

But innovation doesn't end here.

We're entering an era where AI, automation, and emerging technologies will continue to redefine every industry. The frameworks shared in this book were designed to evolve with that future. So revisit them. Tweak them. Share them with your team. Make them yours.

This book was never meant to be the final word — it's your launchpad. The future belongs to those who build it.

Now go. Let's keep building.

Together.

Without drama.

If you're looking for the next step, here's how I can continue to support you:

4.1. A Sneak Peek at the Toolkit I Use

Some of the links are affiliate links, others aren't — but every tool listed here is one I personally use and genuinely recommend.

Innovation Templates & Frameworks
InnovationOS: 1800+ ready-to-use templates to ideate, implement, test, and scale innovation

Survey / Application Forms
Typeform: to collect insights and validate assumptions in minutes

Landing Page A/B Testing
Unbounce: to test different value propositions before investing big

One-Page Websites
Carrd: fast, beautiful landing pages for MVPs or idea validation

Advanced Email Marketing & CRM
ActiveCampaign: to automate outreach and nurture innovation pipelines

Behavior Analytics
Hotjar – to see how users interact with prototypes and digital products

Video Demos & Updates
Loom – quick way to present ideas, align teams, or share progress

4.2. Join my Executive Community

Innovation Hacks:
Stay ahead of the curve with insights, trends, and real-world cases curated for executives.

4.3. Let's Connect

Share your story with me:
I'd love to know how you applied the concepts, the impact you created, and what you've built because of it.

INNOVATION WITHOUT DRAMA

DISCLAIMER

This book is intended for informational and educational purposes only. The author assumes no responsibility for any errors or omissions, or for the use of the information contained herein. All opinions expressed are solely those of the author and do not necessarily reflect the views of any referenced organizations or entities. References to specific companies, brands, or entities in this book are for illustrative and educational purposes only. The author has no affiliation, endorsement, or sponsorship with any mentioned companies, and all trademarks referenced belong to their respective owners. Any case studies, examples, or references to past actions or strategies within specific companies are intended to be illustrative and do not reflect actual events or practices of those entities. These examples are based on the author's personal experiences and are presented as hypothetical scenarios. Readers are encouraged to seek professional advice appropriate to their circumstances before implementing any strategies or concepts discussed in this book. Any resemblance to actual events, persons, or situations is purely coincidental.

www.ingramcontent.com/pod-product-compliance
Lightning Source LLC
Chambersburg PA
CBHW050057230526
45470CB00004B/1570